LANCASTER PAMPHLETS

Hitler and Nazism

Dick Geary

ROUTLEDGE

London and New York

First published 1993
by Routledge
11 New Fetter Lane, London EC4P 4EE

Simultaneously published in the USA and Canada
by Routledge
29 West 35th Street, New York, NY 10001

Reprinted 1994 (twice)

Typeset in 10/12pt Bembo by
Ponting–Green Publishing Services, Chesham, Bucks
Printed in Great Britain by
Clays Ltd, St Ives plc

Printed on acid free paper

British Library Cataloguing in Publication Data
A catalogue record for this book is available from the British Library

Library of Congress Cataloging in Publication Data
Geary, Dick.
Hitler and Nazism/Dick Geary.
p.   cm. – (Lancaster pamphlets)
Includes bibliographical references
1. Hitler, Adolf, 1889–1945.
2. Heads of state–Germany–Biography.
3. National Socialism–Germany–History.
4. Germany–Politics and government–1918–1933.
5. Germany–Politics and government–1933–1945.
6. Germany–Social conditions–1933–1945.
1. Title   II. Series.
DD247.H5G32   1993
943.086'092–dc20   93–18757

ISBN 0–415–00058–0

Contents

Foreword

Lancaster Pamphlets offer concise and up-to-date accounts of major historical topics, primarily for the help of students preparing for Advanced Level examinations, though they should also be of value to those pursuing introductory courses in universities and other institutions of higher education. Without being all-embracing, their aims are to bring some of the central themes or problems confronting students and teachers into sharper focus than the textbook writer can hope to do; to provide the reader with some of the results of recent research which the textbook may not embody; and to stimulate thought about the whole interpretation of the topic under discussion.

Preface

At the end of January 1933 Adolf Hitler was appointed German Chancellor. Within a few months his National Socialist German Workers' Party (NSDAP) – the Nazis – had suspended civil liberties, destroyed almost all independent economic, social and political organisations and established a one-party state. That state persecuted many of its own citizens, at first primarily the Nazis' political opponents, the Communists and Social Democrats. As time passed and with breakneck speed, the doors of the prisons and gates of the concentration camps were opened to take in other 'undesirable' groups in German society: delinquents, the 'work-shy', tramps, homosexuals, freemasons, members of religious sects such as Jehovah's Witnesses, and most notoriously the racial minorities of gypsies and Jews. In 1939 the Third Reich unleashed what became, especially on its Eastern front, a war of almost unparalleled barbarism and slaughter. Whilst the mentally ill and incurably infirm were murdered in the 'euthanasia' programme, various organisations of state, Party and the army embarked upon the attempted extermination of European Jewry. With such a record it is scarcely surprising that the rise of Nazism and the policies of the Third Reich have been subjected to the most massive historical scrutiny. The proliferation of literature has made it almost impossible for the professional historian to keep track of the current state of research and retain some kind of overview. For the lay person the situation is obviously even more difficult.

This Pamphlet is an attempt to organise many of the results of recent research around some of the key themes of Nazi historiography: the role of Hitler himself – a source of heated debate – the factors that brought him to power, the structure and nature of government in the Third Reich, the relationship between that government and the German people, and the origins and implementation of the Holocaust. In such a brief survey certain areas will not be discussed, in particular Hitler's foreign policy and the origins of the Second World War (a topic covered in another Lancaster Pamphlet). The latter omission in certain senses already constitutes a problem; for much of what happened in German domestic politics in this period was inextricably linked to preparations for war. However, such interrelationships will not be overlooked.

I have been fortunate in having as friends some of the most distinguished historians of the Third Reich. In particular I have learnt greatly from the work of Hans Mommsen and that of three colleagues who have died tragically in the last two years – Tim Mason, Detlev Peukert and Bill Carr. Most influential of all has been the contribution of Ian Kershaw, the clarity and profundity of whose research on Nazi Germany is matched only by his wit and good company.

R. J. G. 1993

Glossary and list of abbreviations

BVP	Bayerische Volkspartei (Bavarian People's Party)
DAF	Deutsche Arbeitsfront (German Labour Front)
DAP	Deutsche Arbeiterpartei (German Workers' Party) – a forerunner of NSDAP
DDP	Deutsche Demokratische Partei (German Democratic Party)
DNVP	Deutschnationale Volkspartei (German National People's Party = Nationalists)
DVP	Deutsche Volkspartei (German People's Party)
Freikorps	'Free Corps'. Armed units used to repress revolutionary upheavals in 1918–19
Gau	Nazi Party geographical area, ruled by a Gauleiter, a regional party leader
Gestapo	Geheime Staatspolizei (Secret State Police)
KdF	*Kraft durch Freude* (Strength through Joy)
KPD	Kommunistische Partei Deutschlands (German Communist Party)
NSBO	Nationalsozialistische Betriebszellen-organisation (National Socialist Organisation of Factory Cells)
NSDAP	Nationalsozialistische Deutsche Arbeiterpartei (National Socialist German Workers' Party = Nazis)

Reichskristall-nacht	'Reich Crystal Night' or 'Night of Broken Glass' – 9–10 November 1938 when synagogues and Jewish property were vandalised
Reichstag	the national parliament
Reichswehr	the army in the Weimar Republic
RGO	Rote Gewerkschaftsopposition (Red Trade Union Opposition = Communist union organisations)
SA	Sturmabteilung (Storm Troop)
SPD	Sozialdemokratische Partei Deutschlands (German Social Democratic Party)
SS	Schutzstaffeln (Protection Squads)
Wehrmacht	the armed forces in the Third Reich
ZAG	Zentralarbeitsgemeinschaft (Central Work Community: a forum for employer – trade-union negotiations in the Weimar Republic)

1

Hitler: the man and his ideas

Adolf Hitler was born on 20 April 1889 in the small town of Braunau am Inn on the border of the Austro-Hungarian Empire, where his father was a customs official. After five years at primary school, some time in Linz and experience as a boarder in Steyr the apparently unremarkable Hitler (who never enjoyed his schooling and did not get on too well with his father) moved to Vienna in 1907, a city he had visited the previous year. For a time he made a living selling paintings and drawings of the Austrian capital and producing posters and advertisements for small traders, but his two attempts to gain entry to the Academy of Graphic Arts had failed, leaving the young Hitler an embittered man. Isolated, unsuccessful and with a marked distaste for the ramshackle and multi-national Habsburg Empire. Hitler fled to Munich in 1913 to avoid service in the Austrian army. His flight cannot be dismissed simply as an act of cowardice, for with the outbreak of war in August 1914 Hitler rushed to enlist in the Bavarian army. He served with some distinction, being awarded the Iron Cross on two occasions and promoted to lance corporal in 1917. For him the war was a crucial formative experience. The 'Kameraderie' of the trenches, Germans united against clearly-defined enemies, sacrifice for the Fatherland – these were the values that Hitler was subsequently to contrast with the divisive and self-interested democratic politics of the Weimar Republic. He was in hospital, recovering from a mustard

1

gas attack, when he learnt to his horror of Germany's defeat, the humiliation of the armistice and the outbreak of revolution in November 1918. Henceforth Hitler became a major proponent of the 'stab-in-the-back legend', the belief that is was not the army but the civilian politicians who had let the nation down by signing the armistice agreement. Such politicians were denounced as 'November criminals'.

On leaving hospital Hitler returned to Munich, which experienced violent political upheavals in 1918 and 1919, where he worked for the army as one of many employed to keep an eye on the numerous extremist groups in the city. He soon came into contact with the nationalist and racist German Workers' Party (DAP), led by the Munich locksmith Anton Drexler. It rapidly became clear in the hubbub of Munich beerhall politics that Hitler was a speaker of some talent – at least to those who shared his crass prejudices. In October 1919 he made his first address to the DAP, won increasing influence in its councils and became one of its most publicly prominent members. On 24 February 1920 the organisation changed its name to the National Socialist German Workers' Party (NSDAP). As both this new name and its programme made clear during the year, the party was meant to combine nationalist and 'socialist' elements. The programme called not only for the revision of the Treaty of Versailles and the return of territories lost as a result of the peace treaty (parts of Poland, Alsace and Lorraine) but also for the unification of all ethnic Germans in a single Reich. Jews were to be excluded from citizenship and the holding of office in the new German state, whilst those who had arrived since 1914 were to be deported, despite the fact that many German Jews had fought with honour on the German side during the First World War.

In addition to these staples of *völkisch* (nationalist/racist) thinking, the initial, supposedly unalterable programme of the NSDAP made certain radical economic and social demands. War profits were to be confiscated, unearned incomes abolished, trusts nationalised and large department stores communalised. The beneficiary was to be the small man. Note that this form of 'socialism' did not aim at the expropriation of all private property. Indeed small businessmen and traders were to be protected. Even so, whether these socially radical aspects of the programme, so dear to the heart of Gottfried Feder, the party's

2

'economic expert', ever meant much to Hitler is open to doubt. In any case, by the later 1920s, in efforts to win middle-class votes, this part of Nazism was explicitly disavowed: now only *Jewish* property would suffer. Certainly in the years of Nazi rule between 1933 and 1945 it was precisely the giant corporations like the chemical trust IG Farben which were the major financial beneficiaries.

During this period in Munich Hitler also came into contact with various people who were subsequently to be of great importance to the Nazi movement and some of whom became life-long friends: Hermann Göring, the distinguished First World War fighter pilot with influential contacts in Munich bourgeois society; Alfred Rosenberg, the ideologist of the movement; Rudolf Hess, who had actually served in Hitler's regiment during the war; and the piano-manufacturing Bechstein family. Amongst the most important of his associates at this time was Ernst Röhm of the army staff in Munich, who recruited former servicemen and Freikorps members (the Freikorps had been used to repress revolutionary upheavals on the part of the German left) into the movement and thus established the basis of the SA, the Nazi paramilitary organisation of storm troopers. All these people shared Hitler's view that Germany had been betrayed and was now confronted with a 'red threat'. They held a violent nationalist ardour that often encompassed racism and in particular anti-semitism.

At this time the NSDAP was but one of a plethora of extreme *völkisch* organisations in Munich. By 1923 it had links with the other four patriotic leagues in the Bavarian capital and was also in contact with the disaffected war hero General Ludendorff. Even the Bavarian state government under Gustav von Kahr was refusing to take orders from the national government in Berlin and some of its members wanted to establish a separatist conservative regime free from alleged socialist influence in the Reich capital. This tension formed the backcloth to the attempted Beer Hall Putsch on the evening of 8 November 1923 which ended in farce in the face of a small degree of local resistance and the fact that the Reichswehr, the army, refused to join the *putschists*. In consequence the Nazi Party was banned and Hitler stood trial for his part in the attempt to overthrow the Weimar democracy by force, receiving the minimum sentence of five years imprisonment. This example of the right-wing sympathies of the German judiciary in the Weimar Republic was further compounded by the fact that Hitler, at this stage still not even a German citizen, was given an understanding that an early release on probation was likely. In fact he was released from the prison in the Bavarian town of Landsberg am Lech as early as December 1924, despite the severity of his crime; but whilst in gaol he had dictated to a colleague the text of what became *Mein Kampf* ('My Struggle').[1]

Mein Kampf is scarcely one of the great works of political theory. Its style is crass and was in earlier editions ungrammatical. Free from subtleties of any kind it repeats over and over again the most vulgar prejudices and blatant lies. It uses words interchangeably which in fact mean different things (people, nation, race, tribe) and bases most of its arguments not on empirical evidence but analogies (usually false ones). In so far as the book possesses any structure, the first part is vaguely autobiographical, the second an account of the early history of the NSDAP. As autobiography and history it is full of lies, lies about the time when Hitler first encountered anti-semitic ideas, about his financial circumstances in Vienna – which were nothing like as dire as he would have the reader imagine – and about when he fled from Vienna and when he joined the German Workers' Party. It is important to note, however, that the strange style, the repetition of simplistic argument and often straightforward untruths in *Mein Kampf* was not simply a consequence of Hitler's intellectual deficiencies. In fact he never claimed to be an intellectual and had nothing but contempt for such other-worldly creatures. What he was attempting in *Mein Kampf* was to render the *spoken* word, political demagogy, in prose. This was partly because Hitler was in prison when he dictated the work and therefore unable to address public meetings in person. (In fact the ban on him speaking publicly continued for some time after his release from gaol.) It was also, however, a consequence of his beliefs about the nature of effective propaganda.

A not inconsiderable part of *Mein Kampf* is devoted to reflections on the nature of propaganda. Hitler believed that one of the reasons for British success in the First World War was the fact that their propaganda had been superior to that of the imperial German authorities, superior in its simplicity, directness and willingness to tell downright lies. He had also been influenced by certain ideas about the susceptibility of the masses adduced by theorists such as the American MacDougall and the Frenchman Le Bon. What this thinking added up to was the contention that the masses were swayed less by the written word than the spoken, especially when gathered in large numbers in a public place. The way to win their approval and gain their support under such circumstances was not by reference to a plethora of factual details nor by logical sophistication. Rather the most effective route to the popular heart lay in the perpetual repetition of the most simple and vehement ideas. If you are going to lie, then tell the big lie and do not flinch from repeating it. This argument worked because, to Hitler, the masses were 'feminine' – he could scarcely be described as non-sexist – and swayed not by their brains but by their emotion.

If such reflections explain perhaps a little of the deficiencies of *Mein Kampf* in terms of logic and literary elegance, what, then, of its content? Various issues are picked up in the work in no thorough or genuinely systematic fashion. One of these is the appropriate diplomatic and foreign aims of the German state. Hitler was always adamant that the humiliation of the Treaty of Versailles had to be over-turned and the Reich's lost territories (Alsace, Lorraine, and parts of Poland) returned to Germany. He was also aware that France would never surrender Alsace and Lorraine peacefully. Thus a coming war with France was already implicit in his thinking. However, Hitler's territorial ambitions did not end with the re-creation of the boundaries of Bismarck's Germany. Bismarck, after all, had deliberately excluded Austria and thereby Austrian Germans from the Reich that was created after the victories of 1866 and 1871. In contrast Hitler wanted the pan-German vision of a Reich which would include all ethnic Germans: *ein Volk, ein Reich* (one people, one empire). Despite the ostensible commitment of the US President Wilson and his victorious allies to the self-determination of peoples, such self-determination was denied to the Germans at the end of the First World War. *Anschluss* (union) with the new rump Austrian state was not permitted. At the same time the new states of Czechoslovakia and Poland contained significant German minorities. The ambition to unite all ethnic Germans in a single Reich thus had highly disruptive implications for central and central-eastern Europe.

Even these pan-German aims, however, were not sufficient to

satisfy Hitler. He further believed that the populous German people was being forced to live in a territorial area that was overcrowded and could not meet its needs. Such circumstances bred moral and political decay, especially as many of a nation's best qualities were to be found not in the cities but in the rural areas and amongst the peasantry – what became known as the ideology of *Blut und Boden* (blood and soil). What the German people needed was *Lebensraum* (living space). In turn, of course, this then raised the question: where was such living space to be found? One answer might be in the possession of colonies; but Hitler quickly rejected such a solution. Colonies could not be easily defended and could be cut off from the Fatherland by naval action, exactly as had happened between 1914 and 1918. And any German bid for colonies was likely to antagonise Britain, again the very mistake that the imperial leadership had made before the First World War. Increasingly, therefore, Hitler came to believe that *Lebensraum* would have to be found in the east of Europe and in Russia in particular, where valuable foodstuffs and raw materials were also available. Here then was a programme which implied war in the east. Such a war was to be welcomed in Hitler's view. First, he subscribed to a crude form of social-Darwinism which claimed that struggles and war between peoples were a natural part of history; pacifism he dismissed as a Jewish invention! Second, a war against Soviet Russia would be a holy crusade against bolshevism, a claim that had no little attraction not only to many Germans but also to conservatives throughout Europe. Third, a war against Russia would be a war of superior 'Aryans' (the term Hitler restricted incorrectly to the Nordic peoples) against both inferior Slavs and disastrous Jewish influence – for bolshevism was yet another evil that Hitler considered to be a Jewish concoction. Indeed he believed in the existence of an international Jewish conspiracy which embraced both international Marxism and international finance. Like many fellow anti-semites Hitler thought that the existence of such a conspiracy had been demonstrated by the existence of the document entitled *The Protocols of the Elders of Zion*, which was in fact a forgery on the part of the Tsarist secret police before the First World War intended to distract popular discontent away from the regime and on to the archetypal scapegoat.

The core of Hitler's obsessive beliefs and prejudices was a

virulent racism, a vicious anti-semitism, as set out in the chapter on 'People and Race' in *Mein Kampf*. Here Hitler states that the peoples of the world can be divided into three racial groups: the creators of culture. the bearers of culture (people who are not themselves capable of creating culture but who can imitate the creations of the superior race), and inferior peoples who are the 'destroyers of culture'. Only 'Aryans', a term never precisely defined by Hitler but by which he clearly understands Germanic peoples, are capable of creating cultures, which they do in the following way: small groups of well-organised Aryans, prepared to sacrifice themselves for the communal good, conquer larger numbers of inferior people and bring them the values of culture. (It is worthy of note that 'culture', another undefined term, is created by the sword in this account.) For a time all goes well until the master race begins to mix with its inferiors. This 'sin against the blood' leads to racial deterioration and inevitable decay. As a result Hitler came to believe that the prime role of the state was to promote 'racial hygiene' and to prevent racial intermixing. Subsequently the Nazi state came to embody these eugenic values. Significantly the superiority of the Aryan resides, according to Hitler, not in the intellect – that would have been a difficult position to adopt! – but in the capacity for work, the fulfilment of public duty, self-sacrifice and idealism. In his belief these qualities are not created by society but genetically determined.

For Hitler the opposite of the Aryan was the Jew. Again it is significant that he explicitly denies that Jewishness is determined by religion; rather it is inherited, that is biologically determined. Historically a great deal of European anti-semitism had been generated by the Christian denunciation of the Jews as the murderers of Christ. Unpleasant as the consequences of this religious form of anti-semitism had often been, it none the less meant that Jews who converted to Christianity ceased to be regarded as Jewish in public law. In the pseudo-scientific, biological anti-semitism of the Nazis, such a possibility did not exist: once a Jew, always a Jew. And, for Hitler, being a Jew meant that the individual in question would invariably possess those traits which made the Jew the opposite and implacable enemy of the Aryan: possessing no homeland – what would Hitler have said now? – the Jew was incapable of sacrificing himself for a greater, communal good; he was materialistic and untouched by idealism. Through international finance and international Marxism the Jew attempted to subvert real nations and in fact became parasitical upon them. The use of parasitical analogies reached horrendous proportions in Hitler's thinking: Jews were likened to rats, vermin, disease, the Plague, germs, bacilli. Almost anything that Hitler disliked was blamed on the Jews: the decisions of both Britain and the United States to fight against Germany during the First World War; Germany's defeat in that war; the Russian Revolution; international Marxism; the rapacious banks; and the terms of the Treaty of Versailles. The language used to denounce the Jews is not without significance: if Jews are portrayed in terms unlike *human* beings, they do not have to be treated as human beings. If Jews are 'vermin', then they should be treated as such, that is eradicated.

So far we have seen that Hitler's ideas, as expressed in *Mein Kampf*, already involved the possibility of war in west and east and the policies of racial hygiene and anti-semitism. They also were quite clear on the fact that the Nazi state would not be a democratic state. For Hitler the competition between political parties was scarcely-disguised and self-interested horse-trading. Democratic politics brought out the divisions within a nation rather than its unity and would not prove sufficiently strong to resist the threat of communism. What was needed, therefore, was a strong leader, a *Führer*, who would recognise and express the popular will and unite the nation behind him in a 'people's community' (*Volksgemeinschaft*), in which old conflicts would be forgotten.[2]

The various ideas that appear in *Mein Kampf* have raised two particular questions for historians: first, were such ideas the product of a deranged mind or, if not, what were their origins? Second, did these ideas constitute a programme or plan that was systematically implemented in the Third Reich? In terms of the origins of Hitler's anti-socialist and anti-semitic obsessions or his grand territorial ambitions few serious historians have been prepared – quite rightly – to dismiss Hitler as mad. Much psychological speculation rests on a few shreds of miscellaneous evidence or on none at all. This is not to say that Hitler was not obsessive about certain things, nor that he was never neurotic. He was a hypochondriac and extremely fastidious about his food, becoming a vegetarian in the early 1930s. He was preoccupied with personal cleanliness. Most markedly he possessed

8

an incredible belief in his own rightness and destiny, found it difficult to accept contradiction and had nothing but contempt for intellectuals. He could be enormously energetic at certain points in time, yet was often indolent (with consequences that will be explored later). Somewhat remote, he did not make friends easily but enjoyed the company of women. On the other hand, when he did make friends he remained extremely loyal to them, especially towards those who had been with him in the early days in Munich. It is true that Hitler sometimes appeared to behave in a manic way, shown, for example, in tantrums of rage thrown before foreign leaders or in the clippings seen so often by British audiences of the apparently hysterical public speeches. Much of this, however, was misleading. Hitler's speeches were carefully planned; indeed he practised his gestures in front of mirrors. Furthermore the speeches normally began quietly and slowly. The apparent hysteria of the end was thus planned and instrumental; and the same could be said of many, if not of all, of his tantrums. It is true that towards the end of the war the Führer increasingly lost touch with reality, but considering he was living in remote forests, growing dependent on drugs for the treatment of ailments real or imagined and confronted with by then insuperable problems, this was scarcely surprising. In none of this is there the slightest suggestion of clinical madness.[3]

In any case, one does not need to speculate upon the psychological consequences of Hitler's experience of mustard gas during the First World War or certain physical peculiarities (the failure of one testicle to drop) in order to locate and understand the origins of his ideas, however evil they might be. As Alan Bullock wrote some time ago: 'the political ideas and programme which Hitler picked up in Vienna were entirely unorganised. They were the clichés of radical Pan-German gutter politics'.[4] Sad as it may be, *völkisch* and anti-semitic prejudices were far from uncommon in Austria before the First World War and certainly not the product of the deranged mind of an individual lunatic. In fact it was significant that Hitler came from Austria rather than the more western parts of Germany proper; indeed many of the leading anti-semites in the NSDAP, including the theorist Alfred Rosenberg, who came from the Russian town of Reval, were 'peripheral Germans'. For race was an issue of much greater importance in eastern Europe, where national boundaries did not overlap with ethnic ones. The pan-German movement emerged in Austria in the late nineteenth century under the leadership of Georg von Schönerer, whose ideas had a not inconsiderable impact on the young Hitler. In part pan-Germanism, the demand for a single country for all Germans, was a response of Germans within the Austro-Hungarian Empire to the growing national awareness of other ethnic groups, among them Poles and Hungarians with a historical nationhood, and others such as Czechs and Serbs seeking at the least greater autonomy and in some cases independent nation states. The virulence of popular anti-semitism in eastern Europe was equally a response to the fact that the Jewish presence there was much more marked than in Germany, where there were no huge ghettos and where Jews constituted less than 1 per cent of the total population. Racial hatred was further fuelled in the eastern parts of Europe by the fact that many of the Jews there were unassimilated, dressed distinctly and remained loyal to their own traditions. Hitler's account of encountering a Jew on the streets of Vienna makes great play of the latter's wearing of a caftan and ring-locks.[5]

The extent to which *Mein Kampf* constituted some kind of blueprint for policies later implemented by the Nazis in power is much more problematical. It is the case that Hitler unleashed a world war, destroyed parliamentary democracy and led a state that embarked upon the policies of racial genocide, and thus it is easy to see why many historians have therefore regarded the Third Reich and its barbarism as the inevitable consequences of the views that Hitler had long expressed. Recently, however, some analysts of government in Germany between 1933 and 1945 have moved away from such an 'intentionalist' explanation and have come to stress the 'structural' constraints on policy and the chaotic nature of decision-making; for Hitler was often unwilling or unable to reach decisions, especially where they might have a deleterious effect on his popularity. Against this background, as Ian Kershaw has written, 'Hitler's ideology has been seen less as a "programme" consistently implemented than as a loose framework for action which only gradually stumbled into the shape of realisable objectives'.[6] This debate will be explored at greater length in chapter 3. Suffice it to say here that even if *Mein Kampf* was not a specific programme for a specific course of action – and there are good reasons to doubt it – it was none the less a 'framework for action', often for action on the part of people and agencies who *believed* they were implementing the wishes of the Führer. Otherwise Operation Barbarossa (the invasion of Russia in 1941) and the attempted extermination of European Jewry would be even more incomprehensible events than they are already.

When Hitler emerged from prison in December 1924 his position amongst the various right-wing groups in Germany was relatively strong. His performance at his trial was widely admired in nationalist circles, whilst the Nazi Party was in a state of crisis during his imprisonment, banned by law and lacking strong leadership. Convinced by the dramatic failure of the Beer Hall Putsch, Hitler now realised that the road to power for his movement lay through peaceful means and the democratic process, however long that might take, and even though his ultimate aim was the destruction of parliamentary democracy. This insight he brought to the Party at its re-founding in Munich on 27 February 1925, when the ban on the NSDAP was not renewed. Enhanced as Hitler's status may have been within the extreme right of German politics, however, his position was also confronted with serious challenges. Apart from a series of bitter personal clashes between leading figures in the Bavarian party, the most serious threat came from the Gauleiter of northern and western Germany, under the leadership of Gregor Strasser. They were concerned to stress the socially radical aspects of Nazism and to this end demanded a new party programme. This Hitler saw as a threat to his leadership and at a party meeting on 14 February 1926 in the north Bavarian town of Bamberg he saw off the challenge, stressing his commitment to the original programme and demanding loyalty to the Führer. Henceforth Hitler's position within the Nazi movement was impregnable; and even former critics such as Josef Goebbels were won over. From now on much effort was devoted to the reorganisation of the party and the creation of groups of activists throughout Germany and not only in the large towns and cities. At the same time the few remaining independent *völkisch* groups were swallowed up by the NSDAP.

Despite successes *within* the extreme right, however, Hitler was far removed from the centre stage of Weimar politics. The fringe politics of the Nazi Party held little attraction to the German voter at this point in time. This was demonstrated quite

11

clearly in the Reichstag elections of 1928. The NSDAP gained around 2 per cent of the popular vote in these elections. It did win almost 10 per cent of the vote in some Protestant regions of north-west Germany in 1928, but few could have guessed what significance this would have for the future. The result of the 1928 elections brought to power a coalition government, the so-called 'Grand Coalition', embracing the German Social Democratic Party (SPD) and various middle-class parties. Within two years this coalition had collapsed and thereafter the Reichstag was impotent. At the same time the NSDAP emerged as the largest single party in the country. This massive transformation in the fortunes of the party in such a short period of time suggests that Nazi success was not simply a consequence of the party's propaganda or Hitler's charisma, important as these were, but really depended upon the climate within which Weimar politicians operated.

2

Weimar and the rise of Nazism

Many traditional accounts of the collapse of the Weimar Republic and the rise of Nazism list the host of difficulties which faced the fledgling democracy during its short existence (albeit not as short as that of the Third Reich!) Amongst these were the diplomatic and economic difficulties engendered by the Treaty of Versailles, problems which stemmed from the new constitution, the absence of a democratic consensus, the inflation in the early years of the Republic and the slump at its end. In a sense the problems of the Weimar government just piled one on top of the other until the final straw – or rather final heavy weight – broke the camel's back. Such a traditionalist approach has much to commend it and certainly all the problems listed were real ones. Yet a word of caution should be introduced here, one which will be developed later: not all of these problems were encountered simultaneously. For example the early years of the Weimar Republic witnessed inflation and then the ravages of hyper-inflation, whereas the depression of 1929–33 was *not* a time of rising but of falling prices. This raises some extremely important chronological questions: why was the new state able to survive inflation and not depression? Why did it collapse in the early 1930s and not between 1919 and 1923? And why was the Nazi Party in the political wilderness until the late 1920s? Clearly such questions cannot be answered by a list of difficulties that fails to take into account their timing.

13

There can be no doubt that the Weimar Republic was born under difficult circumstances, indeed in circumstances of defeat and national humiliation. This alone was sufficient to damn it in the eyes of the German right who denounced democratic and socialist politicians for 'stabbing Germany in the back'. The fears of the nationalists were further compounded by the German Revolution of November 1918 and the subsequent emergence of a mass communist movement, whilst their anger knew no bounds when the conditions of the *Diktat* (the dictated terms of the peace agreement) of Versailles became known in the summer of 1919. According to the terms of that treaty the central powers (Germany and Austria-Hungary) were exclusively responsible for the outbreak of war in August 1914 (the so-called 'guilt clause'). Germany was to pay the victorious *entente* powers huge financial reparations, which compounded the country's already vast economic problems. In addition Germany's colonies were handed over to the victors, whilst some of the Eastern territories were ceded to Poland, driving a corridor between East Prussia and the rest of Germany, and Alsace and Lorraine were returned to France. These losses were not just a matter of pride: parts of Silesia incorporated in the new Polish state had valuable lignite deposits. Alsace had a highly developed textile and engineering industry and Lorraine, perhaps most significantly of all, had rich deposits of iron ore that had provided cheap raw material for the steel industry of the Ruhr. The Treaty of Versailles confiscated the German mercantile marine and would have done the same with the German navy had not its sailors scuttled the battle fleet at the Scottish naval base of Scapa Flow. To prevent the resurgence of German militarism the size of the army was also restricted by the terms of the treaty. Finally Versailles did not accord to the German people the same right of self-determination that had been extended to the Poles and the Czechs: Germany and Austria were not allowed to join together, whilst several of the successor states included a German minority amongst their citizens, most notably in the Sudetenland in northern Czechoslovakia. Needless to say, the Treaty of Versailles fuelled nationalist propaganda; and even in the rest of Europe there were those who believed that Germany had been too harshly treated. Such a belief would form the background to the policies of appeasement towards Hitler on the part of Britain and France in the late 1930s.

Faced with these facts, no-one in their right mind would claim that the terms of the Treaty of Versailles did not play a major role in the collapse of the Weimar Republic. It was a constant factor in the rhetoric of the German National People's Party (DNVP) and of the Nazis themselves and was a factor in generating electoral support. Renegotiation of reparations which led to the Americans' Young Plan was cause in 1929 for the Nazis and the Nationalists (DNVP) to join together in the Harzburg Front to denounce the plan and organise a plebiscite against it. This development has often been seen as important for subsequent Nazi success, in so far as Hitler, the extremist fringe politician, was now seen centre stage with leading conservatives and accorded a hitherto unprecedented degree of respectability. Reparations continued to be denounced by some German businessmen as one of the causes of their problems (although in this context it should be recorded that most of the industrial community wanted the Young Plan signed and out of the way) and financial problems engendered by reparations continued to bedevil the formulation of national economic policy. Yet this is not the whole story. Certain questions still remain about the role and significance of the Treaty of Versailles for the survival of Weimar democracy. In the first place, the Nationalists (the DNVP) under their leader from 1928 Alfred Hugenberg were as hostile to the treaty as the Nazis, thus the greater electoral success enjoyed by the latter requires at least some additional explanation. Second, if Versailles was so important, why did the new Republic not collapse earlier, when both the defeat and the treaty were at their most immediate? Why did the political system of Weimar crumble when many of the actual economic problems of reparations were less pressing than in 1923, when the French and Belgians occupied the Ruhr to exact payment forcibly? Why, above all, did coalition governments hold together when dealing with the reparations issue and yet collapse in 1929–30 over a much more mundane issue, that of unemployment benefits and who should pay for them?

Similar reservations can be expressed about another matter that has been held harmful to the health of the Weimar Republic, namely the nature of its constitution. Two aspects of the constitution have been signalled for particular criticism: on the one hand the not insignificant powers accorded to the President of the Republic and on the other the introduction of absolute proportional representation. In the first case the constitution gave the President power to rule by emergency decree (*Notverordnung*) and thus dispense with the need for parliamentary majorities when the country was deemed – and deemed by the President – to be in some kind of danger. With the collapse of the Grand Coalition in 1930, after the Nazis had become the largest party in the Reichstag and after Brüning was appointed Chancellor this is effectively what happened: presidential cabinets governed and their wishes were authorised by the aged and conservative President Hindenburg. Second, the introduction of absolute proportional representation for elections had a number of consequences. If a party could get even 2 per cent of the popular vote it would get 2 per cent of the seats in parliament. Thus small parties, such as the NSDAP in its early days, could get off the ground and survive in a way that would simply not have been possible in Britain under a first-past-the-post system. Furthermore these electoral arrangements encouraged a proliferation of political parties and made it more or less impossible for any one party to obtain an absolute majority in the Reichstag. Government was therefore invariably by coalition and the construction of coalitions none too easy, given the sheer multiplicity of parties with parliamentary seats. All of this is true; but again some words of caution.

The first President of the Weimar Republic, the Social Democrat Friedrich Ebert, had like Hindenburg the power to govern through emergency decree; but he used this power to protect the young state against putsches from the right and insurrections from the left. So the personal and political views of the President are of some importance, independent of the power of emergency decree. In any case the use of these decrees by Hindenburg came after the coalition system had already broken down and it had proved more or less impossible to construct a parliamentary majority. This again leads us back to the question of timing: why did parliamentary government collapse when it did? The answer is not to be found in the constitution. As far as the electoral system is concerned, it is beyond dispute that absolute proportional representation led to the fragmentation of party politics. Yet it is worth remembering that imperial Germany had produced a multi-party system even before the First World War and despite the fact that there was no system of proportional representation then. In fact many parties in the Weimar parliament could claim ancestry from several of these pre-war parties. It is also worthy of note that there were times, especially between 1924 and 1928, when Weimar coalitions did manage to function, albeit with differing degrees of success. Yet again the question of chronology cannot be avoided.

In this context it may not have been so much the number but rather the nature of political parties in the Weimar Republic that really mattered. First, many of the parties were closely aligned with specific socioeconomic interest groups. The SPD, for example, was primarily concerned to represent its mainly working-class membership and electorate and had close links with the trade unions. The German People's Party (DVP) on the other hand was closely aligned with big business interests. This would not of necessity have prevented successful coalition politics in times of economic prosperity or when foreign policy issues predominated. It was fatal, however, in the circumstances of depression, when declining business profitability led the DVP to argue for a relaxation of tax burdens and social welfare payments at the same time that the SPD wanted to see an increase in the size of the state funds to finance benefits for the growing mass of the unemployed. It was precisely the inability of these two parties to agree on this issue of the funding of unemployment relief that caused the Grand Coalition to collapse in 1929–30, ushering in the period of presidential rule.

A second aspect of German party politics boded ill for the stability of parliamentary democracy in Germany after the First World War. Quite simply many parties never accepted the democratic system from the start. The Nationalists looked back nostalgically to the semi-autocratic state of the imperial period, whilst the DVP was prepared to work within the system but was never committed to it as a matter of principle. The German Communist Party (KPD) denounced Weimar democracy as a capitalist sham, to be overthrown by proletarian revolution. Only the labour wing of the Zentrum, the Catholic Centre Party, a broad-based alliance of Catholics with varying social backgrounds, the German Democratic Party (DDP), a middle-class liberal party but one which became increasingly insignificant, and the SPD were fully committed to upholding the democratic system. From 1928 onwards the situation became even more dire in terms of the absence of a democratic consensus. The DNVP became even more reactionary under the leadership of Hugenberg, the national leadership of the Centre Party also moved to the right, and the DVP contained elements who preferred government by presidential cabinets rather than the democratic process.

Another factor which contributed little to the survival of the Weimar Republic was perpetual economic and financial difficulty. The first economic problem was occasioned by the end of the war and the transition to a peace-time economy. The demobilisation of some seven million soldiers and the running-down of the war industries created unemployment. In the winter of 1918–19 over a million Germans were without jobs. Compared to levels of unemployment that were achieved later this figure does not look very high; what was important, however, was that the unemployed were concentrated, at least according to the official figures, in relatively few large cities (over a quarter of a million in Berlin alone in January 1919) which were politically extremely volatile. There is some evidence that some of those who participated in the so-called Spartacist Rising (a left wing insurrection) in Berlin in early January 1919 were jobless. More important, though, and to a degree that was truly remarkable, was the rapid disappearance of unemployment in the post-war boom. Now the problem in economic terms changed: Germans were confronted first with very high levels of price inflation and then with stupendous hyper-inflation. Between 1918 and 1922 prices rose at a rate that often outstripped rises in nominal wages; thus the purchasing power of many declined and this formed the background to a massive wave of strikes between 1919 and 1922 and the rise of extreme left-wing politics. The hyper-inflation of 1923, however, was something else again. Money became worthless, not even worth stealing. Those on fixed incomes – pensioners, invalids, those dependent on their savings, *rentiers* – were ruined. And although those on wages fared somewhat better, as wage rates could be adjusted, prices still rose faster than pay. It is not surprising, therefore, that inflation has often been seen as the nail that sealed Weimar's coffin. It certainly alienated some of its victims from the system permanently. Yet here again the question of the timing of the Republic's collapse becomes relevant.

Despite attempted right-wing *putsches* in Berlin and in Munich in 1920 and 1923 respectively, despite communist attempts to seize power in 1919, 1921 and 1923 in various parts of Germany, and despite the havoc wrought by inflation and hyper-inflation, the Weimar Republic survived. When it collapsed, in the early 1930s, the problem in economic terms was *not* inflation. By then prices were actually falling. This suggests that the inflationary period was not one of unmitigated disaster for all Germans. Working out who won and lost from the inflation is far from easy; for many people were both debtors (beneficiaries as the inflation wiped out their debts) *and* creditors (losers as inflation meant they could not reclaim the real value of what they had loaned to others). Although there can be no doubt that there were real losers, in particular those on fixed incomes, it is equally true that there were some whose position was helped by price inflation. This was especially true of primary producers. Although the farming community complained about many things between 1919 and 1923, particularly government attempts to control food prices, it none the less stayed away from right-wing extremist politics in the early years of the Republic in a way that was not matched after 1928, when the Nazis notched up some of their first and most spectacular electoral successes in the rural areas of Protestant Germany. Part of the reason for this was that both large landowners and small peasant farmers saw their incomes rise between 1919 and 1922 with high food prices. For them it was falling agricultural prices in later years that were to prove a disaster.

Interestingly big business did not regard the inflationary period with unmitigated horror either. Inflation wrote off the debts they might have incurred in earlier borrowing from the banks. The fact that the price of goods rose faster than nominal wages effectively reduced relative labour costs; whilst the devaluation of the mark on international money markets as a consequence of inflation meant that German goods were very cheap on foreign markets and foreign goods extremely expensive in Germany. The result was high demand at home and abroad. Ironically the inflation prolonged Germany's post-war boom to 1923, whereas the boom had ended in Britain and France by 1921. A further consequence was that German business enjoyed very high levels of profitability until 1923 and some leading industrialists such as Hugo Stinnes actually encouraged the Reichsbank to print more paper money. (This inflationary strategy had the further advantage that the reparations set out in the Treaty of Versailles were being paid off in a devalued, almost worthless currency.) High business profitability also had consequences in the field of industrial relations. Forced to recognise trade unions in the wake of the 1918 Revolution and afraid of the threat of a more through-going socialist revolution, employers were prepared to make concessions to organised labour of a kind unimaginable before 1914, when most leading industrialists had adopted authoritarian attitudes and refused to deal with trade unions. In the changed circumstances after the war agreements were reached on union recognition, national wage rates and a shorter working day. Trade-union leaders and business representatives met in a forum called the Central Work Community (ZAG). Although such cooperation was imposed by fear of outside intervention it was also made possible by the high levels of profitability enjoyed by leading companies in these early years of Weimar.

So paradoxically the inflation did not ruin the farming community and in many ways it was not detrimental to the interests of big business. Things only got out of hand when the rate of inflation overtook the international devaluation of the mark in 1923. This, together with the crisis caused by the occupation of the Ruhr, led to a massive collapse in the second half of the year, in which many firms went bankrupt and others were forced to lay off large numbers of workers. In the winter of 1923/4 this so-called 'stabilisation crisis' saw unemployment rise to over 20 per cent of the labour force, which in turn led to an increase in political radicalism and a great upturn in the fortunes of the German Communist Party.

The years 1924 to 1928 used to be regarded as the 'golden years' of the Weimar Republic. Germany was admitted to the League of Nations and the foreign policy of Gustav Stresemann earned international recognition and respect. Inflation was conquered and economic output grew. The extreme right figured nowhere in mainstream politics in these years and coalition government did not seem to be a complete disaster. Yet historians have become increasingly aware of a series of problems that characterised these years as not so much golden as 'tarnished'. On the economic front Germany's recovery had become disturbingly dependent upon foreign loans, on American capital in particular. This meant, of course, that the country was exceptionally vulnerable to movements on international money markets and highly dependent on the confidence of overseas investors. The Wall Street Crash of October 1929 made this fragility abundantly clear. Agricultural prices which had begun to stabilise after the early 1920s were already falling by 1927 and collapsed in the depression of 1929–33. The result was a crisis of indebtedness for farmers, whose alienation from the Republic was already forming in the 1926–8 period. This agrarian crisis formed the background to a campaign of rural violence against tax-collectors and local government and led to the first significant gains of the NSDAP in the agricultural areas of Schleswig-Holstein and Lower Saxony in 1927–8. These somewhat unexpected gains led the Nazis and Hitler to reconsider their strategy: much propaganda had previously been directed at the urban working class, but with little reward. Although the NSDAP did not abandon agitation in the towns it did switch its emphasis away from workers. In the towns the middle class was now targeted; but above all there was a concentration on rural areas and agricultural problems, which reaped huge dividends in the election of 1930.

Nor was everything rosy in the industrial sector in the mid-1920s. Heavy industry (coal, iron and steel) was already experiencing problems with profitability and even in the relatively prosperous year of 1927 German steel mills worked at no more than 70 per cent of their capacity. The disaffection of iron and steel industrialists was demonstrated quite clearly in the following year, when a major industrial dispute took place in the Ruhr and the employers locked out over a quarter of a million workers. If some sections of big business were not exactly satisfied with their economic situation even in the mid-1920s, the same could also be said of some sections of German labour. It is true that the real wages of workers increased in the period 1924–8, but these gains were made at a certain cost. The introduction of new technologies associated with serial production (conveyor belts) meant an intensification of labour, an increase in the pace of work and an increase in the number of industrial accidents. Even where no thorough process of technological modernisation took place – and this was true of most industries – work was subjected to increasingly 'scientific management', a development sometimes described as 'Taylorism'. This meant increased controls of how workers spent their time on the shop-floor, an increase in the division of labour and again a speeding-up of work processes. Associated with this economic 'rationalisation' was the closure of small and inefficient units of production. A consequence of this development was the onset of *structural* as well as the usual seasonal and cyclical unemployment. After 1924 many were without jobs, even in the years of apparent prosperity: the annual average number of registered unemployed stood at over 2 million in 1926, 1.3 million in 1927 and nearly 1.4 million in 1928. Politically the major beneficiary of this fact was the KPD, which remained strong in many industrial regions such as the Ruhr and Berlin even in the supposedly 'good' years.

The onset of the world economic crisis in 1929, however, made the problems of Weimar's middle years almost seem trivial. Agricultural indebtedness reached endemic proportions; and the Nazi promises to protect agriculture against foreign competition, to save the peasant and lower taxes fell on ready ears. Big business entered a crisis of profitability, which made it increasingly antagonistic to welfare taxation and trade-union recognition. Now it could not afford, or so it claimed, the wage levels and concessions it had been prepared to make in the early years of the Republic, albeit under duress. Attempts to revive the ZAG met with no success. Falling prices dented the viability of many companies and led in some cases to bankruptcy, in others to the laying-off of workers *en masse*. At the nadir of the depression in April 1932 the official figure for the number of unemployed, probably an underestimate, stood at no fewer than six million, that is approximately one in three of the German labour force. The consequences of this situation for the Weimar Republic's working class will be developed in due course. If the discontent of big business was bound to grow during the depression, the same was even truer as far as small businesses were concerned. Without the larger resources of the giant trusts, the smaller operators were especially vulnerable to falling prices. They also felt threatened both by big business and large retail stores, which could undercut them, and by organised labour, seen as responsible for pushing up wages and as a threat to the property owner. These were the fears of the German *Mittelstand*, of small businessmen, shopkeepers, independent craftsmen and the self-employed, and they were exploited with great success by Hitler and his followers: there is little doubt that the Protestant lower middle class provided a solid core of Nazi support.[7]

So far we have seen that the Weimar Republic lived in the

22

shadow of defeat: the Treaty of Versailles, constitutional difficulties, fragmented party politics, the absence of a democratic consensus, and a series of economic problems, of which the last – the depression and its *specific* consequences – probably goes further to explain the precise timing of the collapse of the Republic than anything else. It is all too easy to move from an awareness of this list of difficulties to the belief that the rise of Nazism and the triumph of Hitler were inevitable, that the difficulties led 'Germans' to look for some kind of saviour to lead them out of the morass and found that saviour in the Führer. Yet we must beware of generalisations about Germans. The highest percentage of the popular vote won by the NSDAP before Hitler became Chancellor in late January 1933 was just over 37 per cent in the Reichstag elections of July 1932. Even at this point, therefore, almost 63 per cent of those Germans who voted did *not* give their support to Hitler or his party. So generalisations about 'Germans' which are intended to explain Nazi support simply will not do. Moreover the 37 per cent electoral support in July was not sufficient to bring Hitler to power: in the prevailing system of absolute proportional representation this meant that the NSDAP occupied only 37 per cent of the seats in the Reichstag and thus was not in an absolute majority. What is more, at the time the aged General Hindenburg made it quite clear that he was not inclined to appoint the upstart Nazi leader Chancellor. In addition, and partly as a result of this, the fortunes of the NSDAP went into rapid decline after the July elections. Between July and November the Nazis *lost* two million votes. In fact in the November election of 1932 the combined vote of the Social Democrats and the Communists was actually higher than that gained by Hitler and his followers. With one relatively insignificant exception the Nazi vote continued to decline in local and regional elections before Hitler became Chancellor. Thus his appointment was not the result of the acclamation of a majority of the German people, but rather the result of a series of political intrigues with Conservative elites which will now be discussed.

That only some and indeed not even a majority of enfranchised Germans voted Nazi makes it imperative to discover which groups within the nation were most susceptible to Nazi propaganda and to Hitler's acknowledged talents as a speaker and propagandist. There has been a massive amount of research on this very topic, the social bases of Nazi support, and there are several points on which virtually all commentators are agreed. First, Nazi electoral support was much stronger in Protestant than Catholic Germany, a feature of both urban and rural areas. In urban Catholic Germany industrial workers usually either remained loyal to the Centre Party or switched their vote to the KPD. In Catholic rural areas either the Centre Party or its Bavarian counterpart, the Bavarian People's Party (BVP), remained dominant. Nazi electoral success in Bavaria was largely restricted to Protestant Franconia. (As always, there were some exceptions to the general rule: in Silesia the Nazis did well in the Catholic towns of Liegnitz and Breslau, as they did in rural Catholic areas of the Palatinate.) Second, the NSDAP mobilised a large percentage of the electorate in Protestant rural districts. It made its first gains in such regions, and by July 1932 the scale of its support in such areas indicates that it came not solely from small peasant farmers but other sections of rural society too, such as some large landowners and rural labourers. In general the Nazi vote as a percentage of the total vote was much higher in rural districts than in urban centres. Indeed, the larger the town, the lower tended to be the percentage of the electorate voting for the NSDAP. In July 1932, when the party averaged 37 per cent of the vote in the nation as a whole, its vote in the Ruhr was a good 10 per cent lower.

As far as voting behaviour in the towns was concerned, the Nazis enjoyed more success in small or medium-sized towns than they did in the great conurbations. Again historians are generally agreed that one important element in their electoral support here came from the *Mittelstand*. However, historical research is no longer prepared to accept the old stereotype of the NSDAP as simply a party of the lower middle class. Apart from the rural support described here, analysis of electoral districts in the wealthier parts of Protestant towns and the votes of those who could afford a holiday away from home has indicated that significant numbers of upper middle-class Germans were prepared to cast their vote for Hitler, as least by July 1932. The Nazis also enjoyed considerable support amongst the ranks of white-collar workers, who formed an increasing percentage of the labour force (over 20 per cent by this time) and who were strongly represented in the membership of the NSDAP. Once again, however, old stereotypes have had to be reviewed in the light of research: white-collar workers in the public sector (*Beamte*) were apparently more likely than those in the private sector (*Angestellte*) to give their vote to Hitler. Within the private sector white-collar workers with supervisory and clerical functions, as well as those working in retailing, were more strongly inclined to Nazism than those with technical functions. In general white-collar workers who lived in large industrial towns and came from manual working-class backgrounds were relatively immune to the NSDAP's blandishments and often supported the SPD; whereas those living in middle-class districts of the larger towns, or in small provincial towns and those from non-manual origins were more likely to be Nazi supporters.

Already, therefore, we have seen that Hitler's party had a broad support; and it is worth noting that large numbers of Germans were still employed in agriculture at this time and that the self-employed and white-collar workers were also numerous. We are thus some way towards understanding how the Nazis could achieve a significant percentage of the vote. However, there is yet one more factor in the equation and one that has been hotly disputed, namely the extent of working-class support for Nazism. Despite recent research, to be described in due course (see p. 26), the case remains that the larger and more industrial the town, the lower the Nazi percentage of the vote. In general the larger the number of workers in an electoral district, the lower the Nazis' proportion of electoral support, though this is truer of Berlin, Hamburg and the Ruhr than the Saxon towns. Relatively few former KPD-voters switched to the Nazis, despite a popular stereotype, except possibly amongst the rural labourers, whose voting behaviour was exceptionally volatile. Workers were far less likely to be members of the NSDAP or vote for the party than middle-class elements. When the SPD lost votes in the depression some of these (about 16 per cent of SPD voters in 1930) went to the Nazis in July 1932, but the major beneficiaries of desertions from both Social Democracy and the urban Centre Party were the Communists. Some of these deserters may well have been white-collar-workers. The massive rise in the NSDAP vote between 1930 and 1932 left the combined SPD/KPD vote more or less undented, again suggesting that previously organised workers were more likely to be immune to Nazi propaganda than many other groups in German society. Elections to factory councils and trade-union membership figures further suggest that the working-class Nazi was not typical. The overall results of the factory council elections in 1931 saw only 710 representatives of the Nazi Factory Cell Organisation (NSBO) elected as against 115,671 Free Trade Unionists (SPD-oriented) and 10,956 mandates for the predominantly Catholic Christian trade unions. In January 1933 the NSBO had some 300,000 members, compared with one million Christian and over four million Free Trade Unionists.

This is not the whole story, however. Recent research (in German) by Peter Manstein has suggested a working-class membership for the NSDAP of around 35 per cent (though this still means a gross overrepresentation of upper- and middle-class members). Conan Fischer has demonstrated a large manual working-class presence in the SA; whilst Detlev Mühlberger's survey of several German regions suggests wide variations in working-class membership from one district to another (from almost two-thirds in some places to under one-fifth in others). In general he finds that levels of working-class representation within the NSDAP have hitherto been understated. He does admit, however, that the percentages were likely to be higher amongst rural labourers and in small towns; and it is not insignificant that most of the towns he has looked at are relatively small. The impressive electoral studies (in German) of Jürgen Falter lead to the conclusion that roughly one in four workers voted Nazi in July 1932. Given the number of workers in the population, however, this means a lot of Nazi voters. It does seem clear that the Nazis were able to penetrate significant sections of the German working-class electorate. They were more likely to do so in areas of artisan or cottage industry, as in Plauen in Saxony or Pirmasens in the Palatinate, than in heavy-industrial districts such as the Ruhr or areas of factory production. They were more successful in winning working-class support in rural Germany and small provincial towns than in the big cities. A substantial number of women also voted Nazi in July 1932. What these various groups of working-class Nazi voters had in common was they lacked traditions of union or socialist/communist mobilisation; for the centre of trade-union and left-wing political organisation had remained essentially the large city. The sheer size of these previously under-organised groups of workers should not be overlooked. In the early 1930s agriculture still employed over one-fifth of the labour force and one-third of all those employed in 'industry and handicrafts' were self-employed or worked in firms of under five employees. Cottage industry was still prevalent in shoe-manufacture in Pirmasens and in large parts of the Saxon textile industry, as well as in instrument- and toy-making. And over a half of those registered as 'workers' in the occupational census of 1925 lived in small towns or villages of under 10,000 inhabitants. Thus there existed significant potential for Nazi success without that success undermining traditional working-class support for the SPD or the KPD. The NSDAP also won over another group of workers who had political traditions but not those of the left, namely workers who had voted National Liberal before the First World War and DNVP after it. These tended to be workers who lived in the company housing provided by paternalistic employers, such as the Krupp firm in Essen, who were members of company unions and were tied to the company by insurance schemes and pension benefits.

One final point concerning Nazi success or failure amongst the working-class electorate: the contention that the manual unemployed turned in large numbers to Hitler and his supporters cannot be sustained. In the Ruhr town of Herne the NSDAP did least well in areas of high unemployment, often scoring under 13 per cent of the vote even in July 1932. In such areas the KPD enjoyed enormous success (between 60 and 70 per cent of the vote). In the Reich more generally the unemployed were overwhelmingly concentrated in the large industrial cities, precisely where the Nazis polled less well. Again the work of Jürgen Falter shows the NSDAP achieving little support from the manual unemployed, who were more likely to vote Communist.[8]

The distribution of Nazi support described above raises several important questions. Why, for example, were the Nazis more successful in Protestant than in Catholic parts of Germany? At least part of the answer lies in what has been said about those groups of workers most amenable to Hitler's message: the NSDAP was most successful where it did not have to cope with strong pre-existing ideological or organisational loyalties. Where these did exist, as in Social Democratic and Communist strongholds, it did far less well. The same applied to Germany's Roman Catholic community, strongly represented over decades

27

by the Centre Party (or the BVP in Bavaria). Loyalty to the party was reinforced by a plethora of Catholic leisure organisations which penetrated daily life and also by the pulpit, from which the NSDAP was sometimes denounced as godless. On the other hand Nazi success in Protestant rural and middle-class Germany was facilitated by the fact that political loyalties there were either weak or non-existent. In fact Hitler's message was able to get through because a crisis of political loyalty had already taken place during the mid-1920s in peasant communities in Schleswig-Holstein and Lower Saxony, with peasants deserting the DNVP, and amongst lower middle-class urban groups who left the traditional bourgeois parties and formed a host of specific interest group political organisations. It was from these that Hitler picked up much of his support in the early 1930s.[9]

The issues deployed by Nazi electoral propaganda to mobilise this support were many and various. Of these almost all commentators agree that the most significant were nationalism, the denunciation of the Treaty of Versailles and anti-Marxism, though it should be noted that this last meant opposition not only to the Communists, but also to the SPD, the unions, labour law and welfare legislation. Aspects of this hostility even to welfarism will be discussed in more detail (see p. 31). In most local studies and from the contemporary investigations of Theodore Abel it would appear that anti-semitism did *not* play a major role either in electoral propaganda or as a mobilising factor, despite the horrendous events that happened later.[10] However, if the Nazi appeal had relied solely on nationalist and anti-Bolshevik rhetoric, it is difficult to see why the NSDAP should have done so much better in winning support than the traditional Nationalists, whose message was equally nationalistic and hostile to the socialist threat. Part of the explanation, at least, is that the Nazis were able to combine the usual platitudes of the German right with a populist and anti-establishment message. The party was never implicated in government in the Weimar period and thus escaped the necessity of taking unpopular decisions which even the DNVP had to do on occasion. Its leaders were relatively young and not associated with either the traditional social elite or the political establishment. It also made promises to the small man, to the peasant farmer and small shopkeeper, of protection not only against the Marxists but also against big business and large stores. To big business, on the other hand, it promised the demolition of the Weimar system of industrial relations and the restoration of management's right to manage. To women the Nazis promised the return to traditional moral and family values. Interestingly the parties that thought at least partly in terms of female emancipation – the SPD and the KPD – did least well amongst women voters.

It is clear that the Nazis were often promising different things to different people, sometimes things that were incompatible, especially in terms of economic policy. How was this possible? There were several contributing factors. One was the fact that the main element of electoral campaigning at the time was the local political meeting: there was not the instantaneous national media coverage to which we have become accustomed today. Another was the ease with which the various groups of Nazi supporters described above could unite around the major but general themes of NSDAP propaganda: nationalism, hostility to socialism and the political mess of Weimar, as well as traditional moral and family values. Next, it is important to realise that the impact of that propaganda was not simply the result of Goebbels's skill in exploiting symbols and rallies, great as this was, or of Hitler's undeniable talent as a speaker, or at least as a speaker to those who already shared many of his prejudices. It was also the result of an electoral professionalism manifested in two particular ways: first the fact that the Nazi message reached parts of Germany other parties did not reach; second the targeting of specific interest groups with specific messages. In the first case the NSDAP got its speakers, even some of its major figures on occasion, into rural districts and small towns which had often been neglected by the older political parties. In the second its propaganda section trained its speakers to address local and concrete issues, such as the problems of agriculture in Schleswig-Holstein or the threat to small shopkeepers in Hanover created by the building of a Woolworth's store in the town. Thus its success was not just the result of the mouthing of general slogans or the supposed 'irrationalism' of the masses but also the fact that it addressed the immediate material concerns of many Germans.[11]

With all the support it could mobilise before Hitler became Chancellor the NSDAP still fell short of an absolute majority and, as we have already seen, it entered something of a crisis after July 1932. The myth of the party's invincibility had been shaken, the party was getting short of funds, and, as Goebbels admitted, morale was at a low ebb. Yet by the end of January Hitler was Chancellor. What made his appointment possible was what might be described as a deal between the mass Nazi movement on the one hand – Hitler would never have been taken seriously but for the scale of his electoral support – and key conservative groups and politicians on the other. Formulated in a different way, it was not just Hitler and the Nazis who wanted rid of the Weimar Republic; the same was true of several elite groups who came to play an important role in decision-making between 1930 and 1933. The Revolution of November 1918 had failed to remove from office teachers, bureaucrats, judges and army officers who had served in the imperial period and were never enamoured of the values of parliamentary democracy. Judges handed out derisory sentences to right-wing assassins or conspirators, as in the case of Hitler himself after the Beer Hall Putsch. Teachers in the *Gymnasien* (the German equivalent of grammar schools) and many university professors continued to preach imperial and nationalist values. The relationship between the officer corps and the Republic was strained from the very start, as demonstrated by a right-wing attempt to seize power in 1920, the so-called Kapp Putsch, named after its high-ranking leader; for although the army did not join the putschists, it refused to act against them. The large landowners east of the Elbe, the aristocratic Junker, were no more favourably inclined to the Weimar system and continued to have considerable influence – in particular with President Hindenburg, who was one of their own. With the collapse of coalition government in 1930 and rule by presidential decree, the machinations of these pressure groups became increasingly important and ultimately led to Hitler becoming Chancellor.[12]

It is important to realise, however, that the hostility of Junker and army officers to the Weimar Republic was not just a case of conservative 'traditionalism' but also related to quite modern and material concerns. Hostility to the Weimar Republic within the army officer corps, for example, was often led by younger and non-aristocratic technocrats. Their concern was not the restoration of tradition but the modernisation of the army. For them the problem was that such modernisation was not possible in a political system in which they had to compete for funding with the different claims made by Social Democrats and trade unionists. In short they believed that Weimar was spending too much on welfare and not enough on arms. Equally the worries of large landowners stemmed from the economic crisis and chronic indebtedness that had hit the agricultural community. However, they did not blame international market forces for their problems but rather the Weimar system. Privileged and protected before the First World War, they now had to compete with industrial and consumer interests and found themselves subject to taxation to pay for welfare reform: for the Weimar Republic under Social Democratic and Centre Party influence became a welfare state. It increased invalidity, sickness and pension benefits and introduced a system of unemployment insurance. Council houses were built in great numbers, as were public parks, stadia and baths. These benefits, which accrued primarily to the urban working class, had to be paid for by taxation, which was greatly resented in rural areas. In 1932 German farmers were also worried at the prospects of a bilateral trade agreement with Poland, which would have brought the threat of cheap agricultural imports. Thus the concerns of the influential military and agrarian elites were of a quite concrete nature.[13]

The concerns of the German business community were not dissimilar. The relationship between big business and Nazism has long been controversial but it does seem that certain things can be said with some degree of certainty, especially after the research of Henry Turner. First the NSDAP did not need external funding from industrialists: its own activities were in the main self-financing and money-raising. Second the iron and steel baron Fritz Thyssen, who did provide the Nazis with funds and became a party member, was not typical of the business community as a whole. More typical was the Flick concern, which gave money to virtually every political party apart from the SPD and the KPD as a kind of political insurance. Far more industrial funds found their way to the DNVP and the DVP than to the Nazi Party. Hitler's supporters were more likely to be found amongst small businessmen. All this is true, but questions about the relationship between individual industrialists and the NSDAP were arguably less important than the fact that industry in general became increasingly resentful of and hostile to the Weimar Republic. It claimed that welfare taxation was ruining it and that the trade unions had far too much power. This last complaint related to the fact that employers were obliged to recognise the unions, that collective wage agreements were legally binding and that a system of state intervention in industrial disputes was held to have left wages artificially high. Further legislation imposed certain controls on management and was equally resented. The net result was that most of industry wanted to get rid of the Weimar system, even though it was neither necessarily nor in its majority Nazi. Although the role of business in the political intrigues of late 1932 and early 1933 was probably far less important than that of military and agricultural interests, which carried much more weight with Hindenburg, none the less it represented yet another group in German society that was not prepared to back the Republic in its hour of need.[14]

The ability of various elite and pressure groups to influence decision-making in the last years of the Weimar Republic rested on the fact that parliamentary government had effectively broken down by 1930, that is, actually some time before the Nazi seizure of power. From 1928 until March 1930 Germany was governed by a precarious coalition led by the Social Democrat Hermann Müller but including representatives of the Centre, the BVP, the DDP and even the DVP. This coalition had to handle the impact of the Depression; and increasingly the SPD, influenced by their trade-union allies, and the DVP, strongly associated with certain big business interests, found themselves at loggerheads over economic and financial policy in general and in particular over how the unemployment insurance fund should be supported with such a massive increase in the number of jobless. Essentially, the SPD wished to retain welfare benefits, whilst the DVP thought priority should be given to cutting government expenditure. The consequence of this impasse was the resignation of the Müller cabinet on 27 March 1930. Thus ended the Republic's last parliamentary government; for the focus of decision-making now shifted from the Reichstag to the President, Hindenburg, and to those who had influence with him, in particular General Kurt von Schleicher, who had come to speak for the army in the political arena.

Neither Hindenburg nor Schleicher thought attempts to cobble together yet another unstable coalition sensible in March 1930. They wanted a return to firm and decisive government. As a result the succeeding cabinets of Müller's successor as Chancellor, Heinrich Brüning, did not have to rely on majority votes in parliament to pass legislation – in any case they could not manufacture a parliamentary majority, especially after the NSDAP's and KPD's huge electoral gains in the elections of September 1930 – but they could get the President to sign emergency decrees. In this fashion Brüning pursued policies of cutting government expenditure and cutting back on welfare benefits, policies thought highly desirable by agrarian and business interests. Yet this system of rule by 'presidential cabinets' was fraught with difficulties because of its dependence on the goodwill of Hindenburg and his advisers. As the economic crisis deepened (some would say fuelled by Brüning's deflationary policies), as agriculture became increasingly indebted and shrill in its demands for protection and as most business found itself in a crisis of profitability, so the voices of discontent and of those wishing to unseat the Chancellor became louder. Much of big business was not particularly unhappy with his performance but the barons or iron, steel and coal, especially hard hit by the Depression, thought he had not gone far enough in dismantling progressive labour legislation and welfare taxation. The agrarian lobby, dominated by Junker estate owners, also began to agitate for Brüning's removal, putting the idea in the President's head that a plan to take over insolvent agricultural properties in the Eastern provinces and recolonise them was a form of 'agrarian bolshevism'. At the same time, and perhaps decisively, Schleicher was becoming increasingly disillusioned with Brüning; for although Hindenburg and Schleicher were not enamoured of coalition governments and desired 'strong' rule, they each hoped that such rule would none the less have some kind of popular mandate, which Brüning was manifestly unable to deliver. As a result Schleicher had become involved in a series of behind-the-scenes intrigues to try to obtain such a mandate by involving Hitler and other politicians in discussions aimed at getting some broad 'bourgeois' political front. Although these tortuous negotiations came to nothing in the short term, Brüning's difficulties in commanding support led Hindenburg to demand his resignation. On 30 May 1932 the Chancellor resigned, to be replaced by Franz von Papen, also a member of the Centre Party but way to the right of its general political line.

Politics now took a decisively more reactionary course: Papen cut back on welfare payments quite dramatically, removed previous bans on the SA and dissolved the social-democratic government in the state of Prussia. But although he was probably doing enough to satisfy most conservative circles (and Hindenburg was not keen to remove him from office), Papen, like his predecessor, now ran into problems with Schleicher for his inability to generate a broad popular mandate – especially after the Nazis' spectacular electoral gains of July 1932, when they achieved over 34 per cent of the popular vote. Papen did not see eye to eye with Hitler, and his 'Cabinet of Barons' could only rely on support from the DNVP, DVP and BVP. The backstairs intrigue continued. Schleicher told Hindenburg that the army had lost confidence in the Chancellor and on 2 December 1932 Schleicher himself took over in that position. In his attempts to find the kind of mandate his two predecessors had lacked, the new Chancellor embarked on a series of risky manoeuvres involving talks with trade-union leaders and those on the left wing of the Nazi Party. Needless to say, conservative circles were highly disturbed by these developments, as they were by Schleicher's apparent commitment to reflationary policies to counter the slump. This, and the fact that he too failed in his political intrigues to generate the broad support he needed, left Schleicher vulnerable to the same kind of manoeuvres he had himself practised for so long. Conservatives around Papen were finally able to come to a deal with Hitler offering firm right-wing government with a popular mandate (the large electoral support for the NSDAP). Under these circumstances Hindenburg was finally prepared to see Hitler as Chancellor; and the Nazi leader stepped into this role on 30 January 1933. At the time the Nazis were in a minority in the new Cabinet; and older politicians like Papen thought they would be able to control him.

The intrigues that brought Hitler into office rested on the fact that conservatives and Nazis shared many values – nationalism, anti-communism and dislike of Weimar among them – and because the former believed, quite disastrously, that they would be able to control and harness the Führer. Such collaboration is therefore not surprising. Perhaps more puzzling is that those who were to be the first political victims of the new regime, namely the Social Democrats and Communists, seemed to do so little to prevent the Nazi seizure of power. Generally the responsibility for this has been located in the tragic split between the SPD and the KPD and in the way the two parties spent so much time attacking each other. The Communists believed that capitalism had entered a final crisis, that fascism was a last-ditch effort to maintain the capitalist system, that proletarian revolution was now on the agenda and that all it took to prevent it was the activity of Social Democrats in misleading the working class away from the revolutionary path. Thus the SPD had become a prop of capitalism and as such was denounced as being 'social-fascist'. There is no doubt that this attitude was suicidal and led to a gross underestimation of the Nazi threat. Yet this is only part of the story. Fist of all, it is not true to say that the KPD did not attack the Nazis: indeed, its members bore the brunt of the street fighting. Second, the SPD also underestimated the fascist threat and was equally responsible for the split in the ranks of the German labour movement, initially by its counter-revolutionary behaviour when in government immediately after the Great War and then by the policies adopted by social-democratic police-chiefs towards demonstrations by Communists and the unemployed, most notably on May Day 1929, when demonstrators in Berlin suffered fatalities at the hands of the police.

It is important to realise, however, that the inability of the SPD and KPD to reach agreement resulted not only from the political divisions at leadership level; it was also a consequence of the social and economic fragmentation of the German working class in the wake of mass and long-term unemployment. Increasingly the SPD was a party of older, employed, respectable workers, whilst the KPD was overwhelmingly one of younger, unemployed workers who often lived in districts of high criminality. Unemployment set the unemployed against the employed, younger against older worker, region against region and pit against pit in the competition for jobs. Those with jobs were afraid to lose them; those without were incapable of strike action and as time passed sank into an ever-deeper passivity. Unlike 1920, when the Kapp Putsch had been defeated by a general strike, the Depression offered no such possibility with over six million Germans unemployed. Even if the German labour movement had been united, it is still most unlikely that it could have resisted the Nazi seizure of power with any degree of success, for labour stood isolated not only against the Nazis but against the rest of German society too. In any case it would have been no match for the army.[15]

At the end of January 1933 Hitler was appointed Chancellor in a coalition cabinet which contained only three Nazis and a majority of Conservatives and Nationalists who thought they would be able to control him. The Social Democrats hoped that Hitler's period of office would be short-lived and ended by the following elections. Both sets of hopes were to prove tragically mistaken.

3

The Nazi state and society

When President Hindenburg appointed Hitler Chancellor on 30 January 1933 there were only two other Nazis, Hermann Göring and Wilhelm Frick, in the cabinet. That the Nazis were able to consolidate their power so quickly in the months that followed was in part a consequence of Hitler, as Chancellor and leader of the Reich's largest party, being in the most powerful position. With Hindenburg's support he could rule through emergency decree. The position of Göring as Prussian Minister of the Interior was also crucial – he used his power in Germany's largest and most important state to control police appointments and put an end to any police action against the SA, the SS or the nationalist paramilitary organisation, the Stahlhelm. The position of Hitler was further enhanced by the fact that the Nazis took action against the German left, against Communists and Social Democrats in the first instance, breeding a false sense of security amongst the middle-class parties, which were also agreed upon the politics of national revival.

In February 1933 Hitler got his conservative colleagues to agree to the calling of fresh elections with the promise that they would be the last for a long time. Emergency decrees banned hostile newspapers and political meetings, even before fire burnt down the Reichstag on 27 February. Few historians now believe that the Nazis themselves had organised the conflagration, but they certainly exploited the event, drawing up an emergency decree suspending freedom of the press, of speech and association. Personal rights and freedoms had effectively disappeared and the auxiliary police (consisting of, essentially, SA, SS and Stahlhelm men), which Göring had created, was deployed against the Nazis' political opponents. Astonishingly, despite the atmosphere of terror and intimidation and the virtual impossibility of the KPD and SPD mounting the usual election campaigns, the NSDAP still failed to win a majority of the popular vote. In the Reichstag elections held on 5 March 1933 the Catholic Centre Party vote increased from 4.2 million to 4.4 million, the SPD vote dropped but only by just over 66,000 and although the KPD, which had borne the brunt of Nazi attacks, lost over a million votes, it still won the support of over 4.8 million Germans. Hitler and his party won just under 44 per cent of the total vote, still not a clear majority, but enough to enable him to form a majority in the Reichstag in alliance with the DNVP, which polled 8 per cent of the total votes cast. On 23 March 1933 this majority was used to bring in the so-called Enabling Act, by which Hitler's government could rule without the need for action to be authorised either by the Reichstag or by presidential decree. Coincident with these 'constitutional' changes at the political centre, in the localities the Nazi Party, sometimes on its own initiative, sometimes with official backing, had embarked upon a campaign of violence against its erstwhile political opponents. As Jeremy Noakes has written, 'the "seizure of power" was anything but peaceful'.[16] At the local level Nazis interfered in administration and the course of justice, as well as commercial life. In Brunswick their revenge was especially bitter: KPD and SPD buildings were raided, assets seized and party members beaten up. In some places temporary prisons or 'wild' concentration camps were set up, as in the Vulkan docks in the north German port of Stettin and the Columbia cinema in Berlin, where Communists and Social Democrats were sometimes tortured and murdered.

The combination of central government initiatives and local activism also put an end to the powers of the various *Länder* (the states within Germany that had remained federal in structure until 1933). On 9 March von Epp carried out a coup in Munich, turning out the former administration and replacing it with Nazi Party members. Reich police commissars, appointed by Frick, also removed the old authorities in Baden, Württemberg and

Saxony. Then, in the first week of April, Reich governors took charge in every German state: all eighteen of these were Nazis, most of them Gauleiter. The process of the subordination of the *Länder* to central government was finally completed by legislation which came into effect on 30 January 1934.

Other steps were taken to consolidate Nazi control of state and society. The civil service was purged of political opponents and Jews (with the exception, on Hindeburg's insistence, of those Jews who had served in the Great War). Independent pressure groups and political parties were dissolved or declared illegal. The trade unions were dissolved on 2 May 1933 and their assets seized. In June the SPD was banned. The various middle-class parties, generally in agreement with the violence directed against the left but also intimidated by it, offered no resistance and dissolved themselves in June; the Catholic Centre Party followed suit in July. (The KPD, needless to say, had already been illegal for some time.) Thus by the middle of 1933 and within six months of Hitler becoming Chancellor, Germany was a one-party state. The churches continued to enjoy a degree of organisational independence but in this they were almost unique. The only institution to remain untouched – for the time being – was the army. Hitler was aware that interference here might provoke a serious and possibly fatal challenge to his regime, especially whilst Hindenburg was still alive, and hence he sought to win military loyalty (not that difficult, given many of his aims) rather than to engage the generals in a struggle for power.

The consolidation of Nazi power rested on a mixture of centrally directed constitutional change and outright violence in the localities. Much of that violence was the work of the Nazis' organisation of storm-troopers, the SA, under its leader Ernst Röhm. Much of the thuggery was distasteful to middle-class and elite groups in German society. At the same time personal organisational rivalries within the Nazi movement generated hostility towards Röhm and the SA, as, for example, in the case of the SS and its leader Heinrich Himmler. And the existence within the SA of some radical ideas about social change, some kind of 'second revolution' – albeit none too clearly formulated – caused further disquiet. Most crucially of all the army became increasingly worried by what it regarded as the SA's attempt to usurp its role and authority. The result, and one which stood Hitler in good stead with both the elites and the German public

39

at large, was the so-called 'Night of the Long Knives' on 30 June 1934, when the Gestapo and the SS arrested and shot the leadership of the SA. Thereafter Hitler's position was more or less impregnable. After Hindenburg's death on 2 August 1934 the army swore an oath of personal allegiance to Hitler, the civil service an oath of allegiance to the Führer.[17]

The Nazi state which emerged from these developments was one which would brook no opposition and which not only sought to repress and destroy all alternatives but also to mobilise the minds of the people behind the Führer through active propaganda. The media were taken over by the agencies of Joseph Goebbels's Ministry of Propaganda, which further organised the mass rallies and public celebrations of the Third Reich. The syllabuses of the schools and universities were transformed to reproduce the crude racist and geopolitical views of the Nazi leadership. Works by those of different persuasions were banned and burnt. The civil service, as we have seen, was purged of dissident elements, whilst previously independent pressure groups were taken over by the NSDAP. In place of the unions the German Labour Front (DAF) was created under the leadership of Robert Ley. In theory this was meant to be an organisation which reconciled the previously conflicting interests of workers and employers. In practice, although it occasionally caused problems for some employers, it became a mechanism for controlling labour (strikes were illegal in the Third Reich). Certainly it did not function as a trade union, for it played no part in the determination of wage rates. Nazi organisations penetrated private as well as public life. To refuse to allow one's children to join the Hitler Youth or the League of German Maidens could be dangerous; whilst various sporting and leisure activities were organised through the 'Strength through Joy' (*Kraft durch Freude*) movement.

The dissolution of *independent* organisations standing between the individual citizen and the state is of the utmost importance in understanding the apparent quiescence of the German people between 1933 and 1945. Even in liberal, pluralist societies the ability of individuals to stand up for themselves often depends on their ability to join together and gain institutional support from pressure groups. The destruction of independent organisations in the Third Reich, a one-party and terroristic state, simply obliterated the necessary framework for action. In this context it is therefore not surprising that the most overt forms of resistance to Nazi government came from the army and the churches, that is from places where dissidence could still possess some institutional backbone. The difficulty of dissent was additionally compounded by the fact that the Nazi system rested upon what can legitimately be described as institutionalised terror. In the Third Reich civil liberties ceased to exist. There was no recourse to the – in any case Nazified – courts against the actions of the NSDAP, the SA, the SS, the Labour Service or the Wehrmacht. The slightest show of dissent was likely to be met with a beating, with arrest and imprisonment or with incarceration in a concentration camp. The first such camp was erected at Dachau just north of Munich as early as March 1933. Its first inmates were Communists and Social Democrats. As time passed, however, Germany's concentration camps took in ever more social groups deemed by the Nazis to be 'undesirable': anti-social elements, the 'work-shy', freemasons, members of small religious sects and most notoriously the ethnic minorities of gypsies and Jews. The Third Reich repressed its potential enemies with comprehensive and systematic brutality. The lowest number of persons held in concentration camps (and therefore not including those imprisoned for political offences) during the regime's history was 7,500 in the winter of 1936/7. Between 1933 and 1939 12,000 Germans were convicted of high treason. During the war a further 15,000 were condemned to death. The treatment of Communists was especially vicious: of just over 300,000 KPD members in January 1933 over half were imprisoned or sent to concentration camps, whilst no fewer than 30,000 were murdered by the Nazis.[18] The Third Reich witnessed what Ian Kershaw has described as the 'subjugation of legality'. There were large numbers of arbitrary interventions in the legal process. The amalgamation of the police with Himmlers's SS guaranteed a further erosion of legal processes, whilst many actions which lacked legal foundation, such as the execution of the SA leadership in 1934, were justified only retrospectively.[19]

It is not the intention here to claim that Hitler's position in the Nazi state rested exclusively on terror and intimidation: as we will see later, many aspects of policy enjoyed real popular support. But any attempt to assess the relationship between people and government in the Third Reich which ignores the

41

oppression documented above clearly will not be satisfactory. That oppression was successful not only because of its comprehensive and even 'anticipatory' nature – people could be arrested *before* they had done anything – but also because it was based on a systematic and ubiquitous surveillance of the population. The Nazis and Hitler in particular were obsessed with public opinion. Hence the massive information-gathering activities of the Secret State Police (Gestapo). In every block of flats 'block leaders' reported on the views of the residents, on every factory floor stewards had a similar role. Most insidious of all was the way in which spying could even intrude into the family, as portrayed brilliantly by one of the scenes in Bertolt Brecht's *Furcht und Elend des Dritten Reichs* (*Fear and Misery of the Third Reich*). Children indoctrinated in the Hitler Youth or the League of German Maidens could and did report the views of their parents to Nazi officials, who became an alternative source of authority to the parent, priest or schoolteacher. Indeed some witnesses have memories of the period as one in which family ties were disrupted, generation set against generation.[20] Thus those harbouring dissident opinions in Nazi Germany lived in fear of denunciation (often exploited by neighbours and former workmates or colleagues to settle old and often personal rather than political scores). Deprived of civil liberties, they had no independent organisations to represent them and faced imprisonment or incarceration in concentration camps should their dissent take any public form.

In such a manifestly dictatorial state and one in which the *Führerprinzip* (leadership principle) was meant to be embodied, it might seem logical to imagine that government and administration functioned easily: Hitler, the Führer, gave the orders, and these were then transmitted downwards and enacted by the relevant authorities. There is no doubt that when Hitler wanted something he got his way. Equally some of the most momentous decisions made in the Third Reich, especially in foreign policy and military matters, were made by Hitler and no-one else. He was behind the decisions to reoccupy the Rhineland in 1936, *Anschluss* with Austria in 1938 and the invasion of both Czechoslovakia and Poland in the following year. However there is now a body of research which suggests that the processes of German decision-making between 1933 and 1945, especially with regard to domestic policy, were much more complicated, even, at least in some cases, chaotic. In the first place when the Nazis came to power they did not fuse the institutions of the Party and the state administration, in contradistinction to what happened in Russia in part after the Bolshevik Revolution. Thus there existed side by side institutions of the old bureaucracy and of the NSDAP. As far as foreign policy was concerned, for example, the Foreign Office under the direction of the conservative Konstantin von Neurath until 1938 faced competition from the Party's Joachim von Ribbentrop, who offered personal advice to the Führer. In the localities the agencies of regional administration often found themselves at odds with the party's powerful Gauleiter, whose access to the person of Hitler going back to the early days of the Nazi movement gave them considerable authority. The dualism of party and state apparatus was not the end of complexity in the government and administration of the Third Reich. In economic policy there was competition, especially relating to manpower and materials, between the Ministry of Economics, the Wehrmacht, the Gauleiter and, increasingly, Göring's Office of the Four Year Plan, which built up a massive organisational empire employing over a thousand officials. This Office, established on Hitler's instruction in 1936, typified a development that characterised the Führer's style of rule, namely the creation of institutions independent of both the NSDAP and the state bureaucracy to fulfil specific tasks but whose power often then expanded mightily. In addition to Göring's Office of the Four Year Plan there existed the Todt Organisation, subsequently taken over by Albert Speer, to deal with public works, the Hitler Youth under the leadership of Baldur von Schirach, and most infamously of all the hugely powerful empire of the police and the SS, who also took over responsibility for the concentration camps, under the direction of Heinrich Himmler and Reinhard Heydrich. In many ways these various bodies came to resemble personal fiefdoms owing allegiance only to the Führer, their powers circumscribed by no set of rules. During the war and with the conquest of Eastern Europe after 1939 these fiefdoms competed for the spoils of domination and their leaders are perhaps best described as competing 'warlords'.

It is crucial to realise that the different organs of party, state and the *ad hoc* bodies described above did not stand in any hierarchical relationship to one another: there was no rational,

bureaucratic chain of command, nor were areas of responsibility clearly defined or demarcated. All certainly owed allegiance to Hitler, as head of state, party leader or their patron
and creator, but for the most part they followed their own
ambitions and interests. Thus decision-making in the Third
Reich often began in an uncoordinated way and was not the
simple result of directives from a central administration, though
it is true that all the organisations claimed to be working
towards the same goals as the Führer and would never have
frustrated his wishes. This strange fragmentation of policy
formulation and implementation was also evident in the conduct
of the Reich Chancellery. Hitler had little interest in formal
cabinet meetings of ministers and the number of such meetings
declined from 72 in 1933 to only six in 1937 and just one in the
following year. As a consequence policy could not be formulated as the result of discussion between Hitler and his ministers. The only figure that provided contact for the ministers with
one another and between the various ministries and the Führer
was the Head of the Chancellery, Hans-Heinrich Lammers. He
received draft legislation from the ministries and presented it to
Hitler for authorisation. The system, or rather the absence of a
system, thus had a hugely paradoxical consequence: on the one
hand the Führer was all-powerful, the only source of real
authority and linchpin of the system, yet on the other he was
rarely involved in the day-to-day discussions which led to the
formulation of policy. How could such a strange situation have
come about?

A possible explanation and one that has been suggested by
several historians is a highly 'intentionalist' one: Hitler designed
the overt competition between the various agencies of state and
party in order to strengthen his own unique position, in order to
'divide and rule'. There can be no doubt that the ability to play
off state bureaucrats against Gauleiter, or Göring against
Himmler, did give Hitler exceptional power, as we have seen
already. It would also be odd if a person as astute and opportunistic as he had not realised the advantages that accrued from
such a set of informal and unregulated arrangements. However,
the real explanations for the emergence of 'polycratic' or fragmented, multi-institutional decision-making in the Third Reich
are to be found elsewhere – in the nature of the Nazi assumption
of power, the structure of the Nazi Party and the charismatic

44

roots of Hitler's position as Führer, first within the NSDAP and subsequently within the German nation at large. Unlike the Bolsheviks in Russia, the Nazis in Germany did not come to power by overthrowing the old elites in a revolutionary upheaval but rather in collusion with them. Thus Hitler had to tread warily, at least in the early days of the regime, in his dealings with big business and in particular with the military establishment. Both these groups exerted not inconsiderable influence, as witnessed in the 'Night of the Long Knives', for some time, although the period 1934 and 1937 did see a steady increase in power and influence of those closest to the Führer (Göring, Himmler, the Gauleiter) and a diminution in the authority of those (such as the state bureaucracy) who were more distant. In 1938 there was a decisive breach with the older order, as we will see.

A second cause of the complexity of power relationships within Germany after 1933 related to the nature of the NSDAP itself. The Party had been created for the sole purpose of propaganda and the winning of elections. It did not possess the organisational structures or ability to administer a modern state. Hence the continued existence of the former bureaucratic organs of state. Perhaps even more significantly, the NSDAP's total and devoted commitment to its Führer, the sole source of authority and an authority based upon his personal charisma, not upon the hierarchically determined functional role, prevented the development of any bureaucratic-rational delineations of authority below the position of the leader. Thus the Nazi Party already possessed that potential for rivalry and competition for Hitler's support before the seizure of power that became even more marked in the Third Reich itself. The subsequent erosion of legality, the appearance of the Nazi warlords, the competition of leading figures in the regime, were all consequences of the unique position of Hitler himself, the Führer unbounded by constitutional niceties or bureaucratic rules. The behaviour and personality of Hitler thus became a major determinant of the style and indeed content of government after 1933. Initially Hitler performed as Chancellor in the way that the old and punctilious Hindenburg expected of him: he turned up in office hours to discharge his duties. After the General's death in August 1934, however, things changed quite dramatically. Hitler would stay in bed until late morning, read the newspapers in leisurely fashion, might meet up with Lammers and some senior members of the Nazi Party, but would then go off alone for a ride in his limousine. In fact he spent a great deal of time at his retreat in Berchtesgarten – in Bavaria and away from the Berlin he detested. One consequence of this has already been described, the piecemeal formulation of policy from 'below', from various agencies that coexisted and competed in the Third Reich. A second was that it was sometimes extremely difficult to get a decision out of Hitler: issues were often shelved for a not inconsiderable period of time, as occurred during the economic crisis of 1935–6, when a serious shortage of raw materials and foodstuffs arose. Hitler was especially loathe to intervene where decisions might make him unpopular with the general public; and his retention of massive personal popularity throughout most of the regime's existence reflected this fact.

The absence of clear lines of authority and Hitler's own behaviour thus left a space in which personal conflicts and institutional rivalries flourished; and as each organisation sought to outdo the other in its commitment to the Führer and his aims (always the goal, even if no specific instructions were received from above) a process took place which Hans Mommsen has described as 'cumulative radicalisation'. Power relationships within the Third Reich were never static and the Nazis were never simply content to repress the opposition. The regime possessed an in-built dynamism that led to a significant realignment of forces to the detriment of the old elites but to the benefit of Hitler and the various bodies he had created. In late 1937 the Foreign Office under von Neurath and sections of the army, including Werner Fritsch, its leader, and the Minister of War, Blomberg, voiced concern about Hitler's foreign policy aims, fearing they would precipitate a fatal war. Shortly thereafter, in January/February 1938, it transpired that Blomberg had married a prostitute and an old rumour concerning Fritsch's homosexual past began to circulate again, and Hitler got the chance to act. The ensuing crisis had not been engineered by Hitler, as indicated by his initial shock, but, opportunist that he was, he exploited the affair to bring about a significant shift of forces within the governmental apparatus. A large number of generals were dismissed or pensioned off, the new army leader Brauchtisch, promised greater cooperation with the Nazis, a new chief of the armed forces, Keitel, was appointed, the position of War Minister was scrapped and Hitler personally became commander in chief. Similar changes took place elsewhere: in the Foreign Office Ribbentrop took over from von Neurath and new ambassadors were put in post, whilst the Ministry of Economics was also rendered more malleable. These various developments saw an increase in power of those close to Hitler and constituted a real blow to traditional conservative forces. They also issued in a radicalisation of policy in respect of foreign policy with the Austrian and Sudeten crises, economic preparations for war (which were already leading to serious difficulties as far as manpower, raw materials and capital were concerned), and an escalation of violence against Jews and their property culminating in the *Reichskristallnacht* of the night of 9–10 November 1938, when synagogues were burnt down, Jewish shops plundered and about 30,000 male Jews dragged off to concentration camps. The evolution of Nazi anti-semitic policy and its dreadful consequences is discussed at greater length in the next chapter; suffice it to say here that the excesses of 9–10 November 1938 were followed by the centralisation of policy on this issue in the hands of the SS.[21]

In these various ways there can be no doubt that the Nazis brought about a revolution in the nature of the state and German politics between 1933 and 1945. A much more difficult issue is whether or not they also transformed the nature of German *society* in the same period, whether or not Hitler engineered a 'social revolution', to use David Schoenbaum's phrase. The NSDAP certainly claimed to be creating a new kind of society, what its leaders called a *Volksgemeinschaft* (a 'people's community'), in which the divisions that had previously rent the German nation asunder, divisions, for example, of class and confession, would be overcome and Germans would unite in common purpose behind their leader. This would be a racial but classless community. Whether the Nazis ever achieved this end and certainly whether they were successful in eradicating class and other identities is far from easy to answer and depends in part on what is meant by the terms 'classless society' or 'social revolution'. The remainder of this chapter explores two aspects of this question: first, was there an 'objective' social revolution, that is were indices of class such as property ownership, the distribution of income and patterns of social mobility altered in any decisive direction? And second, even if they were not, did Germans none the less witness a change in mentalities and loyalties in such a way that would give credence to the idea of a social revolution that was at least 'subjective'? Put another way, did they buy the idea of the *Volksgemeinschaft* in their heads and their hearts and abandon traditional allegiances?

If we look at property ownership in the Third Reich there was no fundamental redistribution. Large landowners remained large landowners and the giant industrial trusts enjoyed high profits as the major beneficiaries of the economic growth of the armaments boom of 1936–8. What property was confiscated was Jewish (or, after 1939, that of foreign nationals) and it found its way not into the hands of the small businessman, shopkeeper or peasant farmer but into the empires of the likes of Himmler and Göring. In fact capital became more not less concentrated in the Third Reich. This did not mean of course that the relationship between big business and the state was always an easy one between 1933 and 1945: in return for the destruction of the trade unions and the profits that accrued from lucrative armaments contracts, big business dared not risk non-cooperation with the regime. It had to work under multiple constraints, for the state controlled imports, the distribution of raw materials, and wage and price levels. It also found itself in competition with the massive industrial empire that Göring had built up through his Office of the Four Year Plan and which received priority treatment in the allocation of raw materials. Yet industrialists were not expropriated, their property remained in private hands and some, especially those associated with the giant chemical company IG Farben, benefited enormously from Nazi rule. Profits rose faster than wages, rising by over 36 per cent between 1933 and 1939, whilst the share of wages of the gross national income declined from 57 per cent in 1932 to just over 52 per cent in 1939, indicating a redistribution of wealth *away* from the working class.

Despite Nazi promises to the German *Mittelstand* before 1933, capital continued to become more concentrated after the Nazi seizure of power. In general larger firms were more successful in the competition for labour and raw materials than smaller ones; indeed, the number of independent artisans declined from 1.65 million in 1936 to just 1.5 million three years later. Equally the regime prevented radical attempts to destroy existing department stores, the competitive bane of small shopkeepers. This does not mean, however, that nothing at all was done for artisans and shopkeepers. Special taxes were levied on the large stores and it became illegal to erect new ones, whilst several consumer cooperatives were closed down and restrictions placed on door-to-door sales. Self-employed artisans now needed to be members of resurrected guilds and to possess certificates of qualification. They also benefitted from the increased orders associated with the economic recovery of 1936 to 1938. That more was not done for small business, however, and its relative economic decline was less a consequence of deliberate Nazi policies than the logic of industrial production. The great military power that Hitler wished to create could not be built upon small-scale and relatively inefficient producers, especially where raw materials and manpower were in short supply.

The fate of agriculture was not dissimilar under the Nazis. In their ideology the peasantry was portrayed as the backbone of a healthy Germanic society, one uncorrupted by the evils of urban living. The regime did alleviate some of the farmers' problems (although until 1935 hand-outs were more likely to go to the larger and medium-sized estates than smallholdings), whilst the control of imports and an initial setting of agricultural prices at higher levels offered further relief. However, government control of prices could prove a double-edged sword. In addition farmers could not compete with industrial firms for labour as the gap between agricultural and urban incomes actually grew. A further consequence was that Germany became more and not less urban between 1933 and 1945 as people deserted the countryside to earn higher wages in the towns. The explanation can once again be found not in ideology but economic reality: the shortage of manpower in the boom years 1936–8, and even more so during the war, pushed up wage levels, even under the Nazi controls.

The economic experience of labour in the Third Reich no more produced greater equality. We have already seen that the share of national income taken by wages actually fell during the Third Reich. Without unions and with strikes made illegal, workers' class position could change little: the DAF was not allowed any scope in the setting of wage levels. Within the working class, differences in earnings actually grew, as national and regional wage rates were abolished and payment was made solely according to the 'performance principle' (*Leistungs-prinzip*) on an individual basis. This does not mean, however, that workers simply suffered under Nazism. Payment by results benefited healthy young workers, especially those with a skill, at the expense of the older and less productive. There is general agreement that between 1936 and 1938 the real value of take-home pay grew, although most of this gain can be attributed to the fact that the length of the working day increased rather than to an increase in real hourly wages. The 'Strength through Joy' organisation also provided some groups of workers with decent leisure facilities and holidays for the first time, although again it was mainly white-collar and better-placed manual workers who were the prime beneficiaries. Overall, the relationship between capital and labour remained fundamentally unaltered between 1933 and 1945: firms stayed in private hands, bosses remained bosses and workers remained workers.

The role of women in Nazi society also sheds interesting light on the play between ideology and economic reality in Nazi Germany. It is well known that national socialist theory pro-claimed that the woman's role was in the home: to breed for the Fatherland and care for the husband/soldier. Thus the regime embarked upon a series of measures to encourage women to leave the factories, to marry and to produce: abortion was prohibited; birth-control clinics were closed; access to contra-ceptives was restricted; incentives were given to encourage Germans to marry and have children, whilst greater welfare was also provided for mothers. (Note that this pro-natalist policy did not apply to Jews, nor to those deemed to be 'asocials', hereditarily ill or chronically alcoholic. Women in these cate-gories were subject to a programme of compulsory sterilisation and over 400,000 Germans suffered as a result.) The idea that women belonged primarily in the home explains why the indus-trial mobilisation of the female labour force in Germany lagged behind that of some other countries, even during the serious labour shortage of the war years. Yet ideological purity still had to give some ground to economic necessity: in 1933 almost 5 million women were in paid employment outside the home, whereas the figure had risen to 7.14 million by 1939. Labour shortage and rising wages thus drew many females into indus-trial employment, despite the regime's ideological goals.

One area where deep inroads were made into traditional

social structures, however, was the nature of social mobility. Again it would be wrong to imagine that it became easy to rise through the social scale: business leaders, senior bureaucrats, diplomats, those studying in Germany's universities continued to come from relatively privileged backgrounds. Yet it is only fair to point out that, first, long-term changes scarcely had time to manifest themselves during the brief period of Nazi rule. Second, new opportunities for advancement were opened up by membership of the NSDAP itself: the proliferation of offices in government and party agencies gave some degree of status and influence to Nazis of relatively humble background. Third, the regime dealt a blow to the traditional power of certain elite groups, as witnessed in the aftermath of the 1938 'Blomberg–Fritsch crisis' described above (see page 46). The blow was further reinforced in the wake of the July bomb plot of 1944, when a conspiracy to kill the Führer failed and around 5,000 'conspirators' were executed. Many of those killed bore some of the greatest family names of the Prussian aristocracy, including General von Moltke and the man who planted the bomb in Hitler's lair, von Stauffenberg.[22]

So far we have looked at the changes or absence of such in the economy and society of the Third Reich without discovering a real 'social revolution', except in certain particular areas. Before examining whether some form of 'subjective' transformation of German society did actually take place, some points about the nature of the Nazi economy and its performance need to be made. A popular image exists that Hitler's government co-incided with a solution to Germany's most pressing economic difficulty – mass and long-term unemployment – and ushered in a period of growth and prosperity. While it is true that unemployment did disappear, (albeit only completely with the armaments boom of 1936–8), that real wages increased in the same period, although primarily because people worked longer hours, and that a clear revival of industrial production took place, this is not the whole story. First, the German economy was beginning to show signs of recovery in the second half of 1932, and much of the recovery in 1933 can be put down to programmes initiated by earlier Chancellors. Second, the fundamentals of Nazi economic policy were not breathtakingly original. Budgets were not too imbalanced, high tax levels were maintained and savings encouraged, and the prime goal of reducing unemployment was not to engender inflation, of which Hitler had a great fear. Third, most of the Führer's economic policies were not part of a coherent, long-term plan. Rather, as Harold James has written, they were 'provisional *ad hoc* measures' as 'the geopolitical vision still remained as the ultimate way of resolving difficulties or contradictions'.[23] Fourth, the apparently rapid solution of the problem of unemployment was based less on the creation of real new jobs than on various measures which took people out of the labour market without placing them on the unemployment register. Married women were actively discouraged from seeking jobs and many in employment dismissed. State marriage loans encouraged single women to leave their employment; whilst those – men and women – purged from the civil service in 1933 were not allowed to register as unemployed. Many of the young unemployed males (some 240,000 in 1934) were drafted into the *Reich Labour Service*, whilst the reintroduction of military conscription in 1935 removed even more of them from the job market.

It is also true, as Nazi propaganda never ceased to stress, that the regime embarked on a series of job-creation measures, most famously in construction and road building (the creation of the *Autobahnen*): some 5.26 billion RM were invested in such activities between 1933 and 1935. Yet even here one must be cautious: fewer investment funds were put into road-building in 1934 than in 1927 and until 1935 the same could be said of investment levels in housing and transport. (The explanation is that local authorities had been responsible for much of such activity during the Weimar years, a fact that has often been overlooked by many impressed with Nazi economic performance.) Recovery was not equally rapid across all sectors: only in 1935 did levels of employment in the building industry reach those of 1928. Similarly the production of machine tools only overtook the output of 1928 in 1935.

Jobs were created first through the proliferation of the number of public officials administering the civil service and the various Nazi party agencies and second by increased arms expenditure, although much of this was disguised in the form of work-creation schemes in the early years of the Third Reich. Between 1933 and 1935 5.2 per cent of the German GNP was devoted to rearmament – twice the amount spent on work-creation schemes. The boom of 1936–8 was in every sense of the phrase an 'armaments boom', which did much to remove the problem of unemployment but nothing to modernise the German economy or cure its structural defects. By 1939 the economy was suffering from a shortage of skilled manpower, materials and capital. Consumer goods had recovered and manufacturers increased production by lowering the quality of their products, not by technological change. Many of the savings for investment were created by artificial exchange rates, price controls and restricting the share of national income taken by wages. The German economy only became a new economy after 1945.

The inequalities of wealth, property ownership and life chances that continued to exist in Nazi Germany make it difficult to speak of any kind of fundamental change in social structure in 'objective' terms. But that is not the end of the matter, for it is possible to argue that the Nazis did succeed in creating their *Volksgemeinschaft* in subjective terms, that the Germans did unite behind Hitler and that traditional divisions and loyalties were overcome. Thus Nazi ideology and propaganda papered over the real economic and social cracks. Such, indeed, is the claim of David Schoenbaum and others. The idea that the Nazis were successful in this regard obviously implies a change in the values and beliefs of millions of Germans; and it is here that the problems begin. Just how do we know what 'Germans' were thinking and feeling between 1933 and 1945? In this context one simply cannot ignore the terroristic nature of the Nazi state and its ubiquitous surveillance of the population, nor the fact that the Ministry of Propaganda under Goebbels controlled all forms of public expression. Without unions or independent pressure groups to represent them Germans who dared overtly to criticise the regime faced the threat of prison, concentration camp, violence at the hands of the SA, the SS and the Gestapo, and even of death. Under such circumstances it is highly misleading to construe the relative absence of overt opposition or resistance (and in fact there was far more of both than is often imagined) as tacit acceptance of or agreement with the aims of party and government in the Third Reich.

The pressures against dissent were reinforced by two other factors. When the Nazis came to power in 1933 approximately six million Germans were without work. Despite the inducements that led many women to leave the factories and thus open up jobs for men, despite the reintroduction of military conscription and the creation of the Labour Service, in which six months' service was compulsory for young adult males, and despite the 'massaging' of the unemployment statistics (an activity scarcely unique to the Nazis), there were still two million jobless at the beginning of 1936. Only in the subsequent boom was unemployment eradicated. This level of unemployment could be manipulated by the state and the NSDAP: opponents of the regime did not find it easy to find a job, whilst those in the Hitler Youth or the Nazi Party received preferential treatment. This was one of the factors that led to such a massive expansion in the size of the two organisations after January 1933. At that point in time the Hitler Youth had a mere 55,000 members, yet by the end of the same year almost half of German youth aged between 10 and 14 years had joined the organisation and over four million were members by the end of 1935. The NSDAP witnessed similar expansion, increasing its membership by 200 per cent between January 1933 and the end of 1934. By 1939 it had no fewer than five million members. Obviously there could be many reasons for this rush to join, but there is no doubt that for many job prospects and opportunism were the driving force. The second factor that reinforced the hold of the Nazis on German society was the advent of the Second World War in 1939. To resist government in time of war could be construed not simply as opposition to particular policies but as treason; and in any case the terroristic nature of the regime became even more marked during the conflict. The number of crimes which warranted the death sentence was now increased from three to forty-six and over 15,000 such sentences were meted out by the courts of Germany during the war.

This is not to claim that the Third Reich was based exclusively on repression. A range of its policies met with approval from large sections of German society. It does mean, however, that any reconstruction of what ordinary men and women thought of their Nazi rulers is far from easy and that silence must not simply be construed as acceptance. The relationship between the government and the German people from the standpoint of certain specific groups demands examination. In this we are aided by two relatively unusual sources: the intelligence reports of the Gestapo and those of the SPD in exile (the so-called SOPADE reports). Both sets of reports are sufficiently nuanced to carry some degree of conviction and even more remarkably, given their totally different origins, they are often quite similar in their conclusions concerning the state of popular opinion between 1933 and 1945.

An analysis of the relationship between the army and government in the Third Reich demonstrates several traits that could be found in other groups and institutions in the Third Reich. First, there was a whole series of policies with which the High Command could identify more or less totally. These included the attack upon Communists and Social Democrats, the stress on traditional family and moral values, the destruction of divisive Weimar politics, increased military expenditure, rearmament, the reintroduction of conscription and the restoration of national greatness through the undermining of the provisions of the Treaty of Versailles. These reflected the values that the Nazis shared not only with the Wehrmacht but with the German middle class at large. Tensions between the NSDAP and Hitler on the one hand and the army on the other first became marked when the Führer interfered in military matters; or when leading generals such as Ludwig Beck came to fear that Hitler's foreign policy would lead to defeat, as they did in 1936 over the remilitarisation of the Rhineland in defiance of Versailles and two years later in the case of *Anschluss* with Austria and the Sudeten crisis. (This opposition had little to do with a principled opposition to Nazi policy or morality but might best be construed as military self-interest.) In any case Beck's plans fell to pieces when Britain and France appeased Hitler over Czechoslovakia and strengthened the position and prestige of the Führer. Much of the origins of opposition to Hitler within the army during the war stemmed from similar motives: resentment at Hitler's meddling in military matters and the fear that such meddling would lead to defeat. However, there also emerged within the army what might be described as a more moral and principled opposition, one which became disgusted by the barbarism of Nazi rule. This opposition, which included Moltke and Stauffenberg, had contacts with like-minded elements within the churches and even with some socialists, and played a major role in the attempt to blow up Hitler in 1944.

A similar mixture of institutional self-interest, agreement with certain aspects of Nazi policy and yet also principled opposition was to be found in the German churches. The Evangelical (Lutheran) Church had a long tradition of obedience to political authority and had strong historical links with the conservative Prussian state. It detested socialism, identified with the Nazis' stress on traditional moral and family values and in no way resented the passing of the sinful and materialistic Weimar Republic. It also gave full support to the restoration of national pride. Yet attitudes towards the regime and its policies within the Protestant Church were far from united. There were some, calling themselves 'German Christians', who gave full support to the system and who have been described as the 'SA of the Church'. They believed that Christianity was essentially a Nordic religion that had been corrupted by Jewish influences (more than a few problems here with the historical figure of Christ!), that Germans had a divine mission and that the 'Jewish Problem' had to be solved. Such strange fellows, however, were not typical of the Evangelical Church as a whole. On the one hand, in general the church hierarchy sought to avoid conflict with the regime without endorsing all aspects of its policies – not unlike the position of the churches in many parts of Eastern Europe before 1989. On the other, and not unlike the army, it became disquieted when Nazis of a more radical and pagan persuasion attempted to interfere in its internal affairs. There was also within the ranks of German Protestantism a principled opposition which denounced the brutality, godlessness and racism of Nazi rule and established the 'Confessing Church' (*Bekennende Kirche*), whose most famous representative was the pastor Dietrich Bonhoeffer, who became involved in active resistance to Hitler. Thus there was no one Protestant attitude towards government in the Third Reich but a mixture: acceptance of some policies but the rejection of others. It is most definitely not the case that the Nazis succeeded in destroying the confessional allegiance of German Protestants. When, for example, in 1934 two Protestant bishops were arrested, there were angry demonstrations for their release.

The allegiance of the Catholic Church in Germany to Hitler and his regime was even more problematical, given its commitment to Rome, though the rapid signing of a Concordat between the papacy and the Third Reich on 20 July 1933 eased relations. Again the Catholic Church could identify with Nazi attacks on Communists and Social Democrats. It supported the emphasis on traditional morality and shared much of the Nazi view of the role of women and the family in German society. It too had regarded the pluralist and divisive democracy of Weimar as less satisfactory than some form of corporate state, as advocated in a papal encyclical of 1931. However, Nazi anticlerical campaigns in 1936–7 and 1941, interference with its schools and youth organisations and the harassment of its priests also and again generated institutional opposition to the government. On some issues that opposition possessed a moral dimension, most famously in the case of the Nazis' policy of euthanasia: this was explicitly denounced from the pulpit by Archbishop von Galen of Münster and the regime was forced to abandon the open murder of the mentally and physically infirm (the euthanasia campaign did continue, but in private). Some Catholic priests such as Alfred Delp also became involved in the resistance to Hitler that led to the bomb plot of July 1944. Once again a range of attitudes prevailed; and once again the Catholic community of Germany remained loyal to its church. The arrest of popular priests, attempts to remove crucifixes from school classrooms and other forms of interference met with popular outcry in areas that were solidly Catholic. There were demonstrations, mothers refused to send their children to school and threats were made not to pay taxes. In such situations the local NSDAP was often forced to back down.

The army and the churches provide the most obvious examples of overt dissent and opposition in the Third Reich. This is no accident: in both cases organisations with some limited degree of autonomy had continued to exist and thus could provide an institutional backbone and collective support for acts of dissidence. Hence their prominence. In the case of the German working class, on the other hand, the institutional framework for collective resistance had been utterly destroyed. Gone were the unions and those enormous political parties (the KPD and SPD) with their ancillary educational and leisure organisations. It was also the German working class which, with the notable exception of the racial minorities, bore the brunt of Nazi violence and repression. And yet by far the largest number of Germans arrested, imprisoned and incarcerated in concentration camps for acts of political opposition were workers. Both the KPD and the SPD continued their underground opposition to the regime throughout its existence and re-emerged after 1945. (Interestingly it was not the Nazis but the Cold War which killed off the Communist Party, which still recorded support from over 20 per cent of the electorate in some of the towns in the Ruhr in the British zone of occupation shortly after the war.) Of course most workers did not become involved in the dangerous pursuit of active resistance, but most historians concur that the government was never successful in winning their active support. Rather they retreated into private life, into sullen apathy and resignation.

From Gestapo reports and those of the SPD in exile it is clear that there was widespread discontent over food prices in 1935 and early 1936. There were even some strikes amongst those building the *Autobahnen* in 1935 in spite of the consequences of such illegal protest. The constraints against collective action, however, were sufficiently massive to make it extremely rare. On the other hand there was an increase in acts of industrial indiscipline (slow working, absenteeism) in 1937–8 which worried the government sufficiently for it to criminalise such activity. It is probably wrong to characterise these developments as some form of political opposition, but they do indicate that workers were still aware of their position as *workers* – scarcely surprising – and had not swallowed the myth of the 'people's community'.

Even in the case of German working class, however, this is far from the whole story. There were aspects of Nazi policy that could find a positive resonance even here. Although suspicious of the regime's motives, many workers did welcome the leisure activities and holidays provided by the 'Strength through Joy' organisation. Those who regained jobs after earlier unemployment may well have felt some sense of gratitude to their new rulers. The beneficiaries of payment by results and those who achieved supervisory functions (especially during the war with massive labour shortage and the employment of slave foreign labour) also had some reason not to feel too aggrieved. In this context the generation factor probably came into play. It is fairly clear that older workers who had belonged to the communist and social-democratic sub-cultures were not persuaded by the Nazi message. Conversely, younger workers without such a background, arguably the beneficiaries of the 'performance principle', were generally reckoned to have a more positive image of Nazism. It was through Germany's youth that Nazi ideology and organisation made inroads, for example, into rural communities.[24]

That youth was more susceptible to Hitler's appeal than older generations with class and confessional loyalties seems beyond dispute. Yet even here the Nazis did not have it all their own way. The regime preached against the evils of swing music (American, decadent) and, even worse, jazz (decried as negroid), but this did not stop many middle-class adolescents listening to it. Admittedly the phenomenon of 'Swing Youth' cannot by any stretch of the imagination be described as dissident, but it is yet another indication of the fact the Germany's rulers could not simply rid the population of its likes and dislikes and impose their own views. This point applies even more forcefully to some sections of working-class youth in the large cities, where street gangs with intriguing names (the Navahoes, the Raving Dudes – note the Hollywood rather than Germanic references) were formed. These *Edelweisspiraten* ('Edelweiss Pirates') as they became known, rejected the values of the regime, sang popular American hits and parodied the anthems of the Hitler Youth, an organisation which in any case was becoming less popular as its leadership aged, its structure became more bureaucratic and its activities more militarised. The actions and life-style of these gangs were regarded as sufficiently threatening by the Nazi authorities that over seven hundred gang members were rounded up in December 1942 and several of the leaders hung. In Cologne in 1944 some gang members even teamed up with army deserters, escaped prisoners of war and foreign labourers in armed conflict with the forces of law and order.

Obviously the *Edelweisspiraten* were typical neither of German youth nor of the population at large, but we have already seen enough to realise that there was far from conformity of opinion within the Third Reich and that the population had not been 'brainwashed' into a simple identification with everything Nazi. In general Nazi propaganda both before and after the seizure of power was most successful where it could play upon the traditional prejudices and values of German middle-class society, upon issues such as nationalism, anti-socialism, family values. Sadly it has to be admitted that the clearing of the streets of tramps, delinquents and gypsies also could count on a good deal of support from this quarter. But where the regime opposed traditional loyalties, it was far less successful, most obviously in the case of the churches, as also amongst the German working class.

Some aspects of the regime were more popular than others. Whereas the shortages of 1935–6 generated a great deal of grumbling, the relative economic prosperity of 1936–8 saw more positive attitudes towards the government. And although the Nazi Party and its self-seeking functionaries became increasingly detested, the popularity of Hitler reached unprecedented heights. One of the most important reasons for this, of course, was the foreign policy successes that could almost entirely be attributed to Hitler. Yet even here popular opinion was far from one-dimensional. The remilitarisation of the Rhineland, *Anschluss* with Austria and the occupation of Czechoslovakia were popular with the German public not simply because they restored the country's national pride but also because they were won *without war*. All the evidence suggests that there was a widespread fear within Germany of a repetition of the events of 1914–18 and that the initial reactions to the invasion of Poland in early September 1939 were ones of dismay. Thereafter, however, the rapid and relatively bloodless victories of 1939 and 1940 first in Poland then in the West brought Hitler to a pinnacle of personal power and popularity, but fears and anxieties again accompanied the invasion of Russia on 22 June 1941. Subsequent defeats and the intensification of the Allied bombing of German cities obviously led to a deterioration of morale and a loss of faith in the Führer; for that faith had always been predicated upon the most remarkable success. Charisma rarely survives defeat; though even here it has to be said that the front-line troops remained loyal to Hitler, as American interviews at the end of the war made clear.

Amidst the conflicts, competition and rivalries of the Third Reich the 'Hitler Myth' constituted an integrative factor. Created first within the NSDAP itself, then communicated to the German people at large, mainly through the massive activities of Goebbels's Ministry of Propaganda, it fed above all off the foreign policy and military victories of 1936–42. It gathered momentum from the fact that Hitler represented a national unity and apparent harmony that had been so notoriously lacking in the days of the Weimar Republic. Additionally, Hitler was seen as a man of the people, one who did not put on the airs and graces assumed by Göring and who was above the corruption and self-interest that characterised so many in the Nazi Party between 1933 and 1945. Somewhat curiously he was even regarded by many in German society as a representative of law and order (an image which gained hugely from the destruction of the SA leadership in the 1934 'Night of the Long Knives') and as a moderate in contrast to the thugs who were responsible for direct violence against people and property.[25]

The Third Reich erected a system of repression and domination that became ever more radical in the implementation of its aims. During the Second World War it was revealed in its full and barbarous colours, as the few constitutional and legal constraints that had survived – and they were few indeed – were swept away in the nakedness of military occupation and genocide.

4

War and destruction

In the course of the Second World War the 'warlord' nature of
the Nazi regime reached its apogee not simply because a war
was being waged (and on the Eastern front a war of almost
unprecedented barbarity) but also because in the newly occupied
territories, especially in Poland and parts of the Soviet Union,
rule or government in the usual sense was replaced by naked
domination and power exercised by the numerous fiefdoms
described in chapter 3 which competed for the spoils of victory.
Most notable of these was the SS empire erected by Heinrich
Himmler. By 1944 there were 40,000 concentration camp
guards, 100,000 police informers, 2.8 million policemen and
45,000 officers of the Gestapo. This expansion was a consequence both of increased repression within Germany during the
war and the extension of concentration camps and their role.
The armed units of the SS (the *Waffen SS*), which played a
disproportionate part in the implementation of the politics of
genocide, recruited a further 310,000 men from ethnic Germans
outside the boundaries of the Reich. Other warlords included
Fritz Sauckel, whose fiefdom dealt with the deployment of
manpower, Robert Ley, in charge of housing as well as chief of
the German Labour Front, Fritz Todt and his successor Albert
Speer, who had control of armaments and munitions, and
Hermann Göring, whose Office of the Four Year Plan spread its
empire over transport, mining, chemical production and price

controls, and plundered occupied Poland. The proliferation and fragmentation of offices, which effectively prevented any co-ordinated economic and military strategy until the very last days of the war, was further compounded by the increased authority of the Gauleiter, whose direct links to Hitler subverted the influence of the state bureaucracy. In fact as the war progressed it was agencies of the party and the Führer's 'special authorities' (Office of the Four Year Plan, etc.) which increased their power at the expense of career bureaucrats. The Gauleiter were en-trusted with many new tasks relating to the war effort at home but also often put in charge of parts of the newly occupied territories.

What gave the Gauleiter and the special agencies their auth-ority was their personal contacts with the Führer, whose power was now absolute. The erosion of traditional governmental structures which permitted the unchecked exercise of such power also took place at the very centre of the Reich. The role of Hans-Henrich Lammers (see chapter 3) was now undermined, especially after the invasion of the Soviet Union, by the rise of Martin Bormann as head of the Party Chancellery. It was Bormann who controlled access to Hitler and often by-passed governmental bodies as far as legislation in the occupied terri-tories was concerned. He also oversaw what information reached Hitler and transmitted his 'decisions' (which often amounted to no more than casual remarks at the dinner table) to various agencies of the party and state for implementation. The utterly informal nature of such decision-making was nowhere more obvious than in the euthanasia campaign.[26] One single instance set this barbarous campaign in motion. A father petitioned Hitler for permission to have his badly deformed child 'put to sleep'. Hitler agreed and had his personal doctor carry out the task. In this way the process of euthanasia began, although the Führer's eugenic beliefs and commitment to racial purity pro-vided the underlying rationale for such action. At the same time he gave the Führer Chancellery the signal that cases like it could be similarly dealt with and subsequently that adults as well as children could be incorporated into the campaign. Chillingly the doctors of Germany's asylums cooperated in providing the Führer Chancellery with a list of names of the deformed and mentally ill. Ultimately 70,000 were murdered in a programme which was deliberately removed from the control of either the

Ministry of the Interior or the health authorities. Some of those responsible were subsequently involved in the extermination of Polish Jews. The inhumanity of the euthanasia programme not only typified the murderous nature of Nazi rule but also its total disregard for due processes of law. No law was ever passed authorising it, no minister consulted about it. It began with a single case and no written authorisation. When Hitler was later called upon to issue some written authorisation, he put down a few lines on his own writing paper and – significantly – back-dated the authorisation to the first day of the war.[27]

Terrorism and racial violence culminated in the attempted extermination of European Jewry. We have already seen what violent anti-semitic prejudices Hitler had expressed in *Mein Kampf* (see page 7). Although the theme was played down in Nazi electoral propaganda before 1933, it re-emerged after that date with the most ghastly consequences. In the spring and summer of 1933 much of the violence of local Nazi Party branches and SA groups was directed at Jews and their property. A boycott of Jewish businesses was organised for 1 April 1933, although interestingly this seems to have had little success with the German public at large. Anti-semitic sentiment within the NSDAP was also marked in 1935 and led to the promulgation of the 'Nuremberg Laws' on 15 September of that year. These laws prohibited marriage and sexual relations between Jews and non-Jews and deprived Jews of their German citizenship. A further wave of anti-Jewish activity was sparked off by Hitler's speech at the 1937 Nazi Party rally in Nuremberg, when he fulminated against 'Jewish Bolshevism'. Further anti-Jewish violence occurred, Jewish businesses were expropriated and anti-semitic prejudice culminated in the *Reichskristallnacht* of 9–10 November 1938, described in chapter 3. The upshot was the transfer of centralised authority for dealing with the 'Jewish Question' to the SS. The intention now was to speed up the deportation of Jews from the Reich, and Adolf Eichmann took charge of this process.

The outbreak of war, which saw a radicalisation of all aspects of Nazi rule, was also accompanied by a radicalisation of policy towards Germany's Jewish community. In fact Hitler had pre-dicted such a development in a speech to the Reichstag on 30 January 1939, when he threatened that the advent of war would end with the annihilation of European Jewry. With the defeat of

Poland, part of that country, known as the General Government under Hans Frank, was transformed into a massive ghetto of 'inferior peoples', to which rounded-up Jews were sent and kept in the most unsanitary, enclosed conditions. An early result for many was death through disease and starvation. Yet this was nothing to what happened in the wake of the invasion of Russia in 1941. The war against Russia was, to use Hitler's own words, a 'war of extermination' in which the army was to cooperate with the security organisations in killing the political commissars attached to the Red Army. Himmler's right-hand SS-man, Heydrich, also issued instructions that Communist Party officials and 'Jews in the service of the state' should be liquidated. As more and more POWs and Jews fell into German hands, the *Einsatzgruppen*, the squads which implemented Heydrich's instructions, became increasingly indiscriminate in their campaign of murder. Now all Jews, not just adult males, fell victim. Subsequently the order was given for the deportation of German Jews to the East: their death sentence. Some of these, deported to Riga, were the first German Jews to be shot. Then, probably in October 1941, came the order for the extermination of Polish Jews (*Aktion Reinhard*). Extermination camps including those at Belzec and Treblinka were built and former members of the euthanasia campaign became involved in preparations for the systematic murder of Jews by gassing. The 'Final Solution' led to the Holocaust, the extermination of millions.

Given Hitler's vicious anti-semitic prejudices, what he had written in *Mein Kampf* and the content of his Reichstag speech of January 1939, it is not surprising that the 'Final Solution' has been seen as the logical and inevitable outcome of the Führer's intentions. I suggest that there are two reasons why such a view is rather too simple: first, many of the anti-semitic actions in the Third Reich were not necessarily initiated at the political centre, and second, it is far from clear that the 'Final Solution' as it actually occurred, that is the systematic extermination of Jews, was always the ultimate goal. These remarks are in no way intended to absolve Hitler's personal responsibility for mass murder. Even where others within the Nazi Party were responsible for anti-semitic initiatives, they always acted with reference to the Führer's wishes; it was, after all, Hitler's 1937 denunciation of 'Jewish Bolshevism' that formed the background to the events that led up to the *Reichskristallnacht*.

Several of the most important decisions, among them the one to include Jewish women and children in the campaign of extermination, required and got Hitler's approval, as did the decision to deport German Jews to the East. Any suggestion that Hitler did not know about or approve of the 'Final Solution' is simply not credible.

This said, however, the actual development of Nazi policy towards the Jews was often a response to initiatives that had begun from below: the organisation of the 1933 boycott of Jewish businesses was an attempt to harness the violence to people and property dispensed by local Nazi groups and the same could be said of the enactment of the Nuremberg Laws in 1935. In a sense, spontaneous and often unpopular thuggery was replaced by more formal and centralised policy. Such was also the case after *Reichskristallnacht*, when responsibility for the Jews was transferred to the SS. Furthermore the vagaries of anti-semitic policy make it far from certain that Hitler and the Nazis already had a distinct view as to how they would deal with the Jews. Until 1937 at least they seemed to place their faith in deportation and enforced emigration; but this strategy proved unsuccessful when countries such as the USA and Britain began to limit the number of refugees they were prepared to accept. The conquest of eastern Europe opened up a new possibility: the deportation of Jews to the Polish ghetto. The sheer numbers involved, however, soon made it clear that the strategy could not succeed. Even after this was recognised some sections of the SS were working on the 'Madagascar Plan', a scheme to deport Jews to the island in the Indian Ocean! In the early, euphoric weeks of the war against the Soviet Union the deportation of Jews to somewhere east of the Urals was still being contemplated; but the logic of a war of 'extermination', the barbarity of the German military effort (some three million Russian POWs were shot), increasing logistical difficulties and the slow down in the advance of the German forces, who found ever more Jews under their control, irreversibly led to murder. In this process it was not just the SS, Nazis and the *Einsatzgruppen* who played a part but also the army itself. Yet, emphatically, none of this would have been possible without the obsessive anti-semitism and anti-Bolshevism of the Führer himself.[28]

For Hitler the war, and in particular the war against Russia, was nothing less than a crusade: a crusade against the restrictions of Versailles, against Marxism and against the Jews. Yet the actual development of German foreign policy between 1937 and 1941 was not simply the consequence of long-term ideological goals and it did involve the opportunistic exploitation of crises not necessarily of Hitler's own making. On 5 November 1937 Hitler had addressed Germany's military leaders in the context of growing economic difficulties (the navy, for example, was facing an acute shortage of raw materials) and a fear that any military advantage the country enjoyed at the moment might soon be eroded. Hitler stated that a war for living space could wait no longer than 1940 and that it would begin with Austria and Czechoslovakia. However, any opportunity that arose before that date might be exploited for the desired aims. Yet *Anschluss* with Austria was triggered off when the Austrian Chancellor Schussnigg unexpectedly called a plebiscite on the issue and when, in response, the German march into Linz received a hugely enthusiastic welcome from the locals. Equally the precise timing of the invasion of Czechoslovakia was a response to Czech mobilization in May 1938, and the invasion of Poland followed the refusal of Britain to accept German diplomatic initiatives. That Hitler acted opportunistically in these various crises is beyond dispute. It is also true that military and economic pressures played at least as great a role as ideological ones. Yet this cannot justify the conclusion that Hitler had no long-term aims of expansion: he did, of course, and that is precisely why he used opportunities in the way he did to expand eastwards. In fact every extension of the front in the Second World War (outside the Pacific area) was the result of Nazi initiative (Poland, Holland, France, Norway, Russia), except in the case of Greece and Albania, where, aware of the potential threat to the Rumanian oilfields, Germany had to bail Mussolini out of his military difficulties. As early as 31 July 1940 Hitler was planning the destruction of Russia in a campaign that was supposed to last no more than five weeks. Once again a great deal of the motivation was diplomatic (the desire to bring Britain to surrender), military (fear of Soviet military expansion) and economic (the fear that such expansion might include the Rumanian oilfields). Again we can see that the Second World War was not simply a consequence of Hitler's ideological obsessions. Once it began, however, the anti-Jewish

and anti-Bolshevik crusade unleashed the horrendous consequences of those obsessions.[29]

The invasion of Russia in 1941 rested on a grossly mistaken
view of that country's resources and military capacity. It led, of
course, to defeat not only of the German armed forces but of
everything that Hitler and his murderous regime stood for. El
Alamein and Stalingrad spelt the beginning of the end; and
Hitler could no longer escape the charge that his was the major
responsibility for the disaster. Under these pressures Hitler's
health deteriorated and with this deterioration came increased
nervous anxiety and depression. He spent more and more time
on his own and increasingly lost touch with reality, as he visited
neither the front nor his German public. Physical illness and
mental depression became even more serious in the aftermath of
the July 1944 bomb plot and the few who had access to the
Führer spoke of one who had aged dramatically in the last years
of the war. One result was that although Hitler's personal
authority was never challenged by any other figures in the
regime, it was an authority exercised in an increasingly arbitrary and infrequent manner: it became more difficult to get a
decision out of him as the Reich fell apart. When Hitler did
intervene in military matters, on the other hand, the benefits
were somewhat dubious. He was not an ignoramus as far as the
waging of war was concerned and had a good memory for
detail. However, he relied too much on his own experience as
an infantryman in the First World War and failed to appreciate
the need for fast rather than heavily armed tanks to combat the
Russians. His preference for offensive rather than defensive
weapons also led to vast expenditure on the V1 and V2 rockets
and a failure to develop defensive rocketry that might have been
deployed against the Allied bombing raids which flattened so
many of Germany's major cities. Here the concentration of
power in Hitler's hands was clearly dysfunctional for the war
effort. Yet the disaster, when it came, was no simple consequence of a series of individual and mistaken military decisions:
it was implicit in the Nazi programme of military expansion
and genocide from the very start. Germany simply did not
possess the resources of geopolitical supremacy (a point that
became even clearer after the entry of the USA into the war in
December 1941).

Surrounded by ruins, increasingly volatile in his moods and

determined that no part of *his* Germany should outlive him (he had ordered a scorched earth policy in the face of the Allied advances) Hitler committed suicide in the bunker of the Reich Chancellery in Berlin on 30 April 1945. Within a few days the Third Reich capitulated and ceased to exist.[30]

Conclusion

It is dangerous to see in the collapse of the Weimar Republic and the rise of Hitler some kind of German peculiarity. Democracies collapsed all over Europe between the wars. Furthermore, fascism was endemic, though its strength varied enormously from one country to another. Hitler's views mirrored those of many of his contemporaries in central and eastern Europe, where ethnic resentments smouldered. The strength of racist feeling has been made only too clear since 1989. Yet Hitler's ability to mobilise popular support at the end of the Weimar Republic, although he failed to win over the majority of the electorate before he actually came to power, was also a consequence of specifically German problems too, in particular the absence of a democratic tradition in that country and the multiple problems of the new Republic described in chapter 2. Even here, however, the evidence suggests that voters were swayed less by irrational prejudices than by their immediate material interests and difficulties. This explains why Weimar collapsed when it did, that is, in the Depression of 1929–33 and not during the earlier inflationary years. The dynamic Nazi movement, populist and not identified with the system, was then able to collaborate with other right-wing groups to bring Hitler to power. Whether either those older conservative politicians and army officers or the Nazi electorate itself had a clue as to what would actually follow is more than a little doubtful.

This last point, of course, raises the terrifying moral issue: how could the people of a supposedly civilised country not simply tolerate but become implicated in the horrific barbarism of the Nazi state, which murdered not only its political enemies but whole categories of 'misfits' and 'outsiders', most notably – but far from exclusively – gypsies and Jews? Part of the answer lies in the terroristic nature of the Third Reich, described in chapter 3, part in the privatisation and retreat of individuals engendered by the destruction of mechanisms of public protest. Yet, most chilling of all, much of what the Nazis did rested upon relatively common and mundane prejudices: dislike of 'outsiders': tramps, gypsies, homosexuals, Communists. Thus although it never succeeded in brainwashing an entire people, the Third Reich could rely on the support of many as far as a good number of its policies were concerned. Some individuals, against all the odds and at risk of life and limb, did resist, indeed far more than is normally imagined. It is to them that this small volume is dedicated.

Notes

1 There are many biographies of Hitler. See the following works in the select bibliography: Bullock (1952, 1991), Fest (1974), Jenks (1960), Kershaw (1991), Maser (1973), Smith (1967), Stern (1974), Stone (1980), and Toland (1976). For the early history of the Nazi Party see Gordon (1972) and Orlow (1971–3, vol. 1.

2 On Hitler's ideas see, apart from *Mein Kampf*, Baynes (ed.) (1942), Hitler (1953), Jäckel (1972), Maser (1970), Rauschning (1939) and Stoakes (1987). On Nazi ideology more generally see Cohn (1970), Pulzer (1964) and Smith (1989).

3 For discussions of Hitler's personality see Carr (1986), Langer (1972), Smith (1967), Stierlein (1978) and Waite (1977).

4 Quoted in Bullock (1952), p. 44.

5 See Pulzer (1964).

6 Quoted in Kershaw (1991), p. 7.

7 On Weimar and its many difficulties there is an enormous literature. See, for example Eschenburg (ed.) (1970), Kershaw (ed.) (1990), von Kruedener (ed.) (1990), Laffan (ed.) (1988), Nicholls (1989), Nicholls and Matthias (1971).

8 For breakdowns of Nazi electoral support see Childers (1983), Childers (ed.) (1986), Hamilton (1982), Larson *et al.* (1980), Mühlberger (1980, 1991) and Mühlberger (ed.) 1987).

9 On the undermining of traditional political loyalties in the mid-1920s see Heberle (1970), Jones (1972, 1986).

10 See Abel (1966) and the statistical breakdown of the same data in Merkl (1980).

11 For general accounts of Nazi propaganda and Goebbels's role therein see Baird (1975), Bramsted (1965), Hale (1964), Heiber (1973), Welch (1983), Welch (ed.) (1988) and Zeman (1964). On the specific targeting of that propaganda towards certain social groups see several examples in Noakes and Pridham (1983–7), vol. 1.

12 An excellent account of the backstairs intrigues which brought Hitler to power is to be found in Bullock (1952).

13 On agriculture see Bessel and Feuchtwanger (eds) (1981), Corni (1990) and Jones (1986). On the army see Carsten (1966) and Gordon (1957).

14 For big business see Geary (1983b, 1990), Schweitzer (1964) and Turner (1985).

15 On labour's failure at the end of the Weimar Republic see Evans and Geary (1987), Geary (1983a, 1990).

16 Quoted in Noakes and Pridham (1983–7), vol. 1, pp. 124ff.

17 On the consolidation of Nazi rule see Kershaw (1991), ch. 3.

18 The terroristic nature of the Nazi state is analysed in Bracher (1973), Buchheim (1968) and Gellately (1990).

19 See Kershaw (1991), ch. 3.

20 The disruption of family ties is described in the chapter by Wilke in Bessel (ed.) (1987).

21 The polycratic, even chaotic, nature of Nazi rule is analysed in Bessel and Feuchtwanger (1981), Caplan (1988), Hirschfeld and Kettenacker (eds) (1981), Kershaw (1991), Mason (1981) and Noakes (1980).

22 On the issue of whether there was a social revolution in the Third Reich see Hiden and Farquharson (1983), Kershaw (1989b), Neumann (1944), Noakes and Pridham (1983–7), vol. 2, and Schoenbaum (1966). On agriculture see Farquharson (1976); on big business see Gillingham (1985), Hayes (1987), Overy (1982) and Schweitzer (1964); on labour see Hoffmann (1974), Mason (1966, 1977, 1992) and Merson (1985); on women see Koonz (1987) and Stephenson (1976). The sterilisation programme is treated in the chapter by Noakes in Bessel (ed.) (1987).

23 James (1986), p. 354. The rest of the account of Nazi economic performance is heavily dependent on this book.

24 On public opinion in general see Kershaw (1983). For the army see Cooper (1978), Deist (1981), Müller (1984) and O'Neill (1966). On the churches see Conway (1978), Erikson (1977) and Helmrich (1979). On labour see Hoffmann (1974), Mason (1966, 1977, 1992), Merson (1985) and Peukert (1987). Youth is dealt with in Peukert's chapter in Bessel (ed.) (1987) and in Koch (1975). The penetration of rural communities by the Nazis is discussed by Wilke in Bessel (ed.) (1987).

25 See Kershaw (1989a).

26 The brutality of Nazi domination is analysed in Kershaw (1991), ch. 6. On the SS see Buchheim *et al.* (1968) and Höhne (1972). On Robert Ley see Smelser (1988); on Speer see Schmidt (1984) and Speer (1970); on Göring see Overy (1984).

27 On the origins of the euthanasia programme see Kershaw (1991) ch. 6.

28 There is a massive and conflicting body of literature on the origins of the Holocaust. See Bauer (1978), Broszat (1987b), Browning (1978, 1987), Cohn (1977), Dawidowicz (1975), Fleming (1986), Gordon (1984), Hilberg (1960), Hirschfeld (ed.) (1986), Marrus (1987), Pulzer (1964), Reitlinger (1968) and Schleunes (1970). For a clear, general account see the chapter by Carr in Bessel (ed.) (1987). For a more thorough survey of the literature see the relevant chapter in Kershaw (1989b).

29 A balanced account of the various motives which informed German foreign policy can be found in Carr (1979) and Kershaw (1991).

30 Hitler's ability as a military commander is discussed in Carr (1986), Schramm (1972) and Strawson (1971). An account of his last days is to be found in Trevor-Roper (1947).

Select bibliography

Abel, T. (1966) *The Nazi Movement* (New York).

Abraham, D. (1986) *The Collapse of the Weimar Republic*, 2nd edn (New York).

Allen, W. S. (1966) *The Nazi Seizure of Power* (London).

Arendt, H. (1958) *The Origins of Totalitarianism* (London).

Baird, J. W. (1975) *The Mythical World of Nazi Propaganda* (Oxford).

Bauer, Y. (1978) *The Holocaust in Historical Perspective* (London).

Baynes, N. H. (ed.) (1942) *The Speeches of Adolf Hitler* (Oxford).

Beetham, D. (1983) *Marxists in the Face of Fascism* (Manchester).

Berg, D. R. (1983) *The Old Prussian Church and the Weimar Republic* (London).

Bessel, R. (1981) *Political Violence and the Rise of Nazism* (London).

—— (ed.) (1987) *Daily Life in the Third Reich* (Oxford).

—— and E. J. Feuchtwanger (eds) (1981) *Social Change and Political Development in the Weimar Republic* (London).

Binion, R. (1976) *Hitler among the Germans* (Oxford).

Bracher, K. D. (1973) *The German Dictatorship* (London).

Bramsted, E. K. (1965) *Goebbels and National Socialist Propaganda* (Michigan).

Broszat, M. (1981) *The Hitler State* (London).

—— (1987a) *Hitler and the Collapse of Weimar Germany* (Leamington Spa).

—— (1987b) 'Hitler and the genesis of the Final Solution', in H. W. Koch (ed.) *Aspects of the Third Reich* (London).

Browning, C. R. (1978) *The Final Solution and the German Foreign Office* (New York).

—— (1987) *Fateful Months* (New York).

Buchheim, H., Broszat, M., Jacobson, H. A. and Krausnick, H. (1968) *Anatomy of the SS State* (London).

Bullock, A. (1952) *Hitler* (London).

—— (1991) *Hitler and Stalin* (London).

Caplan, J. (1988) *Government without Administration* (Oxford).

Carr, W. (1979) *Arms, Autarky and Aggression*, 2nd edn (London).

—— (1986) *Hitler. A Study in Personality and Politics*, 2nd edn (London).

Carroll, B. (1963) *Total War* (The Hague).

Carsten, F. L. (1966) *The Reichswehr and Politics* (Oxford).

—— (1967) *The Rise of Fascism* (London).

Cecil, R. (1972) *The Myth of the Master Race* (London).

Childers, T. (1983) *The Nazi Voter* (Chapel Hill, New Jersey).

—— (ed.) (1986) *The Formation of the Nazi Constituency* (London).

Cohn, N. (1970) *Warrant for Genocide* (London).

Conway, J. (1978) *The Nazi Persecution of the Churches* (London).

Cooper, M. (1978) *The German Army, 1933–45* (London).

Corni, G. (1990) *Hitler and the Peasants* (Oxford).

Dahrendorf, R. (1966) *Society and Democracy in Germany* (London).

Davidson, E. (1977) *The Making of Hitler* (London).

Dawidowicz, L. S. (1975) *The War against the Jews* (New York).

Deist, W. (1981) *The Wehrmacht and German Rearmament* (London).

Deutscher, H. C. (1974) *Hitler and his Germans* (Minnesota).

Diehl, J. M. (1977) *Paramilitary Politics in the Weimar Republic* (Bloomington).

Dorpalen, A. (1974) *Hindenburg and the Weimar Republic* (London).

Eley, G. (1983) 'What produces Fascism?', in *Politics and Society* 12, pp. 57–82.

Erikson, R. P. (1977) 'Theologians in the Third Reich', in *Journal of Contemporary History*, 12, pp. 595–615.

Eschenburg, T. (ed.) (1970) *The Road to Dictatorship* (London).

Evans, R. J. (1989) *In Hitler's Shadow* (London).

—— and D. Geary (1987) *The German Unemployed* (London).

Farquharson, J. G. (1976) *The Plough and the Swastika* (London).

Fest, J. (1972) *The Face of the Third Reich* (London).

—— (1974) *Hitler* (London).

Fischer, C. (1983) *Stormtroopers* (London).

Fleming, G. (1986) *Hitler and the Final Solution* (Oxford).

Fox, J. P. (1979) 'Adolf Hitler. The debate continues', in *International Affairs* 55, pp. 252–65.

Geary, D. (1983a)'The failure of German labour in the Weimar Republic', in M. Dobkowski and I. Wallimann (eds), *Towards the Holocaust* (Westport, Conn.), pp. 177–96.

—— (1983b) 'The industrial elite and the Nazis', in P. D. Stachura (ed.) *The Nazi Machtergreifung* (London). pp. 85–100.

—— (1985) 'Nazis and workers', in *European Studies Review*, xv (4), pp. 453–64.

—— (1990) 'Employers, workers and the collapse of the Weimar Republic', in I. Kershaw (ed.) *Weimar: The Failure of German Democracy* (London), pp. 92–119.

Gellately, R. (1990) *The Gestapo and German Society* (Oxford).

Gillingham, J. R. (1985) *Industry and Politics in the Third Reich* (London).

Gordon, H. J. (1957) *The Reichswehr and the German Republic* (Princeton).

—— (1972) *Hitler and the Beer Hall Putsch* (Princeton).

Gordon, S. (1984) *Hitler, Germans and the 'Jewish Question'* (Princeton).

Grill, J. P. H. (1983) *The Nazi Party in Baden* (Chapel Hill).

Grunberger, R. (1971) *Social History of the Third Reich* (London).

Haffner, S. (1979) *The Meaning of Hitler* (London).

Hale, O. J. (1964) *The Captive Press in the Third Reich* (Princeton).

Hamilton, P. H. (1982) *Who Voted for Hitler?* (Princeton).

Hayes, P. (1987) *Industry and Ideology* (Cambridge).

Heberle, R. (1970) *From Democracy to Nazism* (New York).

Heiber, H. (1973) *Goebbels* (London).

Helmrich, E. C. (1979) *The German Churches under Hitler* (Detroit).

Hiden, J. and Farquharson, J. (1983) *Explaining Hitler's Germany* (London).

Hilberg, R. (1960) *The Destruction of the European Jews* (Chicago).

Hildebrand, K. (1968) *The Third Reich* (London).

Hirschfeld, G. (ed.) (1986) *The Policies of Genocide* (London).

—— and L. Kettenacker (eds) (1981) *The Führer State* (Stuttgart).

Hitler, A. (1953) *Table Talk* (London).

—— (1960) *Mein Kampf*, ed. D.C. Watt (London).

Hoffmann, P. (1974) *The German Resistance* (London).

Höhne, H. (1972) *The Order of the Death's Head* (London).

Holborn, H. (ed.) (1981) *Republic to Reich* (Stuttgart.

Hood, C. B. (1989) *Hitler. The Path to Power* (London).

Hunt, R. N. (1966) *German Social Democracy, 1918–1933* (Princeton).

Irving, D. (1977) *Hitler's War* (London).

Jablowsky, D. (1989) *The Nazi Party in Dissolution* (London).

Jäckel, E. (1972) *Hitler's Weltanschauung* (Middleton, Conn.)

—— (1978) *Hitler in History* (London).

James, H. (1986) *The German Slump* (Oxford).

Jenks, W. A. (1960) *Vienna and the Young Hitler* (New York).

Jones, L. E. (1972) 'The dying middle', in *Central European History*, pp. 23–54.

—— (1986) 'Crisis and realignment in the late Weimar Republic', in R. Moeller (ed.), *Peasants and Lords in Modern Germany* (London).

Kater, M. (1983) *The Nazi Party* (Oxford).

Kehe, H. and J. Langmaid (1987) *The Nazi Era* (London).

Kele, M. H. (1972) *Nazis and Workers* (Chapel Hill).

Kershaw, I. (1983) *Popular Opinion and Public Dissent* (Oxford).

—— (1989a) *The 'Hitler Myth'* (Oxford).

—— (1989b) *The Nazi Dictatorship*, 2nd edn (London).

—— (1991) *Hitler* (London).

—— (ed.) (1990) *Weimar: The Failure of German Democracy* (London).

Kitchen, M. (1970) *Fascism* (London).

Koch, H. W. (1975) *The Hitler Youth* (London).

—— (ed.) (1987) *Aspects of the Third Reich* (London).

Koonz, C. (1987) *Mothers in the Fatherland* (London).

Koshar, R. (1986) *Social Life, Politics and Nazism* (Chapel Hill).

von Kruedener, R. (ed.) (1990) *Economic Crisis and Political Collapse in the Weimar Republic* (Oxford).

Laffan, M. (ed.) (1988) *The Burden of German History* (London).

Langer, W. (1972) *The Mind of Adolf Hitler* (New York).

Laqueur, W. (1979) *Fascism*, 2nd edn (London).

Larsen, U. *et al.* (1980) *Who were the Fascists?* (Bergen).

Lebovics, H. (1969) *Social Conservatism and the Middle Class in Germany* (Princeton).

Leopold, J. A (1977) *Alfred Hugenberg* (New Haven, Conn.).

Maier, C. S. (1988) *The Unmasterable Past* (Cambridge, Mass.).

Marrus, M. (1987) 'The history of the Holocaust', in *Journal of Modern History*, 59, pp. 114ff.

Maser, W. (1970) *Hitler's Mein Kampf* (London).

—— (1973) *Hitler* (London).

Mason, A. W. (1966) 'Labour in the Third Reich', in *Past and Present* 33, pp. 112ff.

—— (1977) 'National Socialism and the German working class 1925–33', in *New German Critique*, pp. 2–32.

—— (1981) 'Intention and explanation: a current controversy about the interpretation of National Socialism', in G. Hirschfeld and L. Kettenacker (eds), *The Führer State* (Stuttgart) pp. 23–42.

—— (1992) *Social Policy in the Third Reich* (Oxford).

Merkl, J. P. (1975) *Political Violence under the Swastika* (Princeton).

—— (1980) *The Making of a Stormtrooper* (Princeton).

Merson, A. (1985) *Communist Resistance in Nazi Germany* (London).

Milward, A. (1965) *The German Economy at War* (London).

Mommsen, H. (1979) 'National Socialism: continuity and change', in W. Laqueur, *Fascism*, 2nd edn (London) pp. 43–72.

—— (1986) ' The realisation of the unthinkable', in G. Hirschfeld (ed.) *The Policies of Genocide* (London).

—— (1990) *From Weimar to Auschwitz* (London).

Mosse, G. L. (1966a) *Nazi Culture* (London).

—— (1966b) *The Crisis of German Ideology* (London).

—— (1975) *The Nationalisation of the Masses* (New York).

—— (1979) *Nazism* (Oxford).

Mühlberger, D. (1980) 'The sociology of the NSDAP', in *Journal of Contemporary History* pp. 493ff.

—— (1991) *Hitler's Followers* (London).

—— (ed.) (1987) *The Social Bases of European Fascism* (London).

Müller, K.-J. (1984) *Army, Politics and Society in Germany, 1933–1945* (Manchester).

Neumann, F. (1944) *Behemoth* (Oxford).

Nicholls, A. (1989) *Weimar and the Rise of Hitler*, 2nd edn (London).

—— and E. Matthias (1971) *German Democracy and the Triumph of Hitler* (London).

Niewyk, D. L. (1980) *The Jews in Weimar Germany* (London).

Noakes, J. (1971) *The Nazi Party in Lower Saxony* (Oxford).

—— (1990) *Government, Party and People in Nazi Germany* (Exeter).

—— (1983) 'Nazism and revolution', in N. O'Sullivan (ed.), *Revolutionary Theory and Political Reality* (London) pp. 73–93.

—— and G. Pridham (1983–7) *Nazism: A Documentary Reader*, 3 vols (Exeter).

Nolte, E. (1964) *Three Faces of Fascism* (New York).

O'Neill, R. J. (1966) *The German Army and the Nazi Party* (London).

Orlow, D. (1971–3) *History of the Nazi Party*, 2 vols (London).

Overy, R. (1982) *The Nazi Economic Recovery* (London).

—— (1984) *Goering. The 'Iron Man'* (London).

Peterson, E. N. (1969) *The Limits of Hitler's Power* (Princeton).

Peukert, D. (1987) *Inside Nazi Germany* (London).

Picker, H. (1974) *The Hitler Phenomenon* (London).

Poulantzas, N. (1974) *Fascism and Dictatorship* (London).

Pridham, G. (1983) *Hitler's Rise to Power* (London).

Proctor, R. N. (1988) *Racial Hygiene* (Cambridge, Mass.).

Pulzer, D. G. (1964)*The Rise of Political Anti-Semitism in Germany and Austria* (New York).

Rauschning, H. (1989) *Hitler Speaks* (London).

Reitlinger, G. (1968) *The Final Solution* (London).

Rosenhaft, E. (1983) *Beating the Fascists?* (Cambridge).

Schleunes, (1970) K. A. *The Twisted Road to Auschwitz* (London).

Schmidt, M. (1984) *Albert Speer* (New York).

Schoenbaum, D. (1966) *Hitler's Social Revolution* (London).

Schramm, P. E. (1972) *Hitler. The Man and Military Leader* (London).

Schweitzer, A. (1964) *Big Business in the Third Reich* (London).

Shirer, W. (1961) *The Rise and Fall of the Third Reich* (New York).

Smelser, R. (1988) *Robert Ley* (Oxford).

Smith, B. F. (1967) *Adolf Hitler. His Family, Childhood and Youth* (Stanford).

Smith, W. B. (1989) *The Ideological Origins of Nazi Imperialism* (London).

Sohn-Rethel, A. (1970) *Economic and Class Structure of German Fascism* (London).

Speer, A. (1970) *Inside the Third Reich* (London).

Speier, H. (1986) *German White Collar Workers and the Rise of Hitler* (New Haven, Conn.).

Stachura, P. D. (1975) *Nazi Youth and the Weimar Republic* (Santa Barbara).

—— (1983) *Gregor Strasser* (London).

—— (1989) *The Weimar Republic and the Younger Proletariat* (London).

—— (ed.) (1978) *The Shaping of the Nazi State* (London).

—— (1983) *The Nazi Machtergreifung* (London).

—— (1986) *Unemployment and the Great Depression in Weimar Germany* (London).

Steinberg, M. S. (1977) *Brownshirts* (Chicago).

Stephenson, J. (1976) *Women in Nazi Society* (London).

Stern, F. R. (1961) *The Politics of Cultural Despair* (Berkeley).

Stern, J. P. (1974) *Hitler* (London).

Stierlein, H. (1978) *Adolf Hitler. A Family Perspective* (New York)

Stoakes, G. (1987) *Hitler and the Quest for World Dominion* (Leamington Spa).

Stone, N. (1980) *Hitler* (London).

Strawson, J, (1971) *Hitler as a Military Commander* (London).

Toland, J. (1976) *Adolf Hitler* (New York).

Trevor-Roper, H. R. (1947) *The Last Days of Hitler* (London).

Turner, H. A. (1985) *Big Business and the Rise of Hitler* (Oxford).

81

—— (ed.) (1972) *Nazism and the Third Reich* (New York).

Unger, A. H. (1974) *The Totalitarian Party* (Cambridge).

Waite, R. G. C. (1977) *Hitler. The Psychopathic God* (New York).

Welch, D. (1983) *Propaganda and the German Cinema* (London).

—— (ed.) (1988) *Nazi Propaganda* (London).

Wheeler-Bennett, J. W. (1953) *The Nemesis of Power* (London).

Woolf, S. (1968a) *European Fascism* (London).

—— (ed.) (1968b) *The Nature of Fascism* (London).

Zeman, Z. A. B. (1964) *Nazi Propaganda* (Oxford).